SPEAKING OF BEAUTY

ALSO BY DENIS DONOGHUE

The Third Voice: Modern British and American Verse Drama
An Honoured Guest: New Essays on W. B. Yeats
(editor, with J. R. Mulryne)
Connoisseurs of Chaos: Ideas of Order in Modern American Poetry
The Ordinary Universe: Soundings in Modern Literature
Jonathan Swift: A Critical Introduction
Emily Dickinson
Jonathan Swift: A Critical Anthology (editor)
William Butler Yeats
W. B. Yeats: Memoirs—Autobiography: First Draft (editor)
Thieves of Fire
Seven American Poets (editor)
The Sovereign Ghost: Studies in Imagination
Poems of R. P. Blackmur (editor)
Ferocious Alphabets
The Arts Without Mystery
We Irish: Essays on Irish Literature and Society
Selected Essays of R. P. Blackmur (editor)
Reading America: Essays on American Literature
England, Their England: Commentaries on
English Language and Literature
America in Theory (editor, with Louis Menand
and Leslie Berlowitz)
Warrenpoint
Being Modern Together
The Pure Good of Theory
The Old Moderns: Essays on Literature and Theory
Walter Pater: Lover of Strange Souls
The Practice of Reading
Words Alone: The Poet T. S. Eliot
Adam's Curse: Reflections on Literature and Religion

Speaking *of* Beauty

DENIS DONOGHUE

Yale University Press   New Haven and London

Published with assistance from the foundation
established in memory of Philip Hamilton McMillan
of the Class of 1894, Yale College.
Set in Caslon type by Tseng Information Systems.
Printed in the United States of America.

The Library of Congress has cataloged the hardcover edition as follows:
Donoghue, Denis.
Speaking of beauty / Denis Donoghue.
p. cm.
Includes bibliographical references and index.
ISBN 0-300-09893-6 (cloth : alk. paper)
1. English literature—History and criticism—Theory, etc.   2. Art and
literature—Great Britain.   3. American literature—History and
criticism—Theory, etc.   4. Ruskin, John, 1819-1900—Aesthetics.
5. Art and literature—United States.   6. Tragic, The, in literature.
7. Aesthetics—Terminology.   8. Aesthetics, American.
9. Aesthetics, British.   I. Title.
PR408.A68 D66 2003
820.9'384—dc21
2002012243

A catalogue record for this book is
available from the British Library.

The paper in this book meets the guidelines
for permanence and durability of the Committee
on Production Guidelines for Book Longevity of
the Council on Library Resources.

ISBN 0-300-10593-2 (pbk. : alk. paper)

10 9 8 7 6 5 4 3 2

Again for Frances

La beauté, "Beauty is difficult, Yeats" said Aubrey Beardsley
    when Yeats asked why he drew horrors
    or at least not Burne-Jones
    and Beardsley knew he was dying and had to
    make his hit quickly

hence no more B-J in his product.

So very difficult, Yeats, beauty so difficult.

    —Ezra Pound, Canto 80, *The Cantos of Ezra Pound*

Contents

Acknowledgments

Some of this material was published in earlier versions in *New Literary History, The Sewanee Review, The Southern Review, The Saint Ann's Review,* and *Ruskin è Venezia: La Bellezza in Declino* (2001). I am grateful to the editors for permission to reprint. Thanks are also due the following publishers and individuals for permission to quote from their books: New Directions Publishing Corporation for lines from *The Cantos of Ezra Pound,* Macmillan for passages from *The Collected Poems of W. B. Yeats* and *The Complete Poems of Marianne Moore,* Alfred A. Knopf for lines from James Merrill's *Selected Poems, 1946–1985* and Wallace Stevens's *Collected Poems,* Harcourt, Inc., and Faber & Faber for lines from T. S. Eliot's "Burnt Norton," Liveright Publications for lines from Hart Crane's "Voyages," Harper & Row for Edna St. Vincent Millay's "Euclid alone has looked on Beauty bare," Indiana University Press for lines from Kenneth Fearing's "Love, 20¢ the First Quarter Mile," Houghton Mifflin for lines from Geoffrey Hill's *The Triumph of Love,* Swallow Press/Ohio University Press for lines from *The Poems of J. V. Cunningham,* and B. H. Fairchild for passages from his "Beauty."

Introduction

I started thinking of writing a short book on the language of beauty when, over a period of several months, I read nothing but Ruskin. Sergio Perosa, a professor of English in Venice, was arranging a conference there and he invited me to give a talk on Ruskin's preoccupation with Venice, beauty, and the city in its decline. I found the idea of decline hard to think about. There seem always to have been happier times, and cultures in better order; at least that is what I am admonished to assume when I read Yeats, Pound, Eliot, and other modern writers. The past is supposedly not only a foreign country but a more admirable one, more intelligently disposed. I was beginning to be skeptical of the notion. But Ruskin was a problem; he seemed increasingly to set the terms of reflection and interest. Beauty is difficult, as Beardsley says in one of Pound's *Cantos*. It seems a self-evident value and to brook no question. It thrives on keeping quiet and never explains itself. I often respond to the beauty of a sentence or a stanza of a poem before thinking about its truth or other value. "In the mountains, there you feel free." "And follow Cupid for his loaves and fishes." ". . . and I left in complex cordiality, loving her, her two men, her dog, and the darkening inhospitable sky which matched my lonesomeness." In a later chapter I try to indicate how I read Ruskin on the subject of beauty, before and after Perosa's conference in Venice. But I also had Yeats's words in mind when I thought of beauty, especially the last stanza of "Among School Children" which is beautiful but doesn't mention the subject, and "Adam's Curse" which is not quite as beautiful but movingly worries the subject.

"Adam's Curse" is one of the first poems in which Yeats, long immersed in visions and dreams, acknowledges the irrefutable force of time in human life. The poem refers to a conversation the poet had in London, one evening in May 1902, with his beloved Maud Gonne and her sister Kathleen. The talk turned to the difficulty of writing poems, the stitching and unstitching of words, and to the labor entailed since the fall of Adam and Eve by anything worth doing. In the background, but tacitly, there was the particular burden of a man's being in love with a beautiful but unresponsive woman such as Maud. Kathleen, perhaps to avoid that theme, said something along these lines:

> To be born woman is to know—
> Although they do not talk of it at school—
> That we must labour to be beautiful.[1]

I don't think she meant merely hairstyling and makeup, hours spent before the mirror. There was more to it: the daily processes of well-being, health, exercise, clothes, jewelry, the achievement of style and expression, voice, demeanor, posture, the adjudged and sustained tone of being in the social world. Women in Kathleen's social class were not expected to do much more. Their teachers did not talk of beauty at school because it was supposed to be a gift of nature rather than a labor and an acquisition. A woman should not have to learn it with the rigor of learning mathematics or a foreign language. Meanwhile, in the public world a society may or may not labor to be beautiful: if it does, it starts by taking care of its people, especially the vulnerable ones, and looks to health services, insurance, sewage disposal, the provision of food, clean air, and pure water. After that, if it has means and taste, it cultivates roses, gardens, domestic and civic styles, cities, towns, parks, décor, design in cars and boats; it builds the Sydney Opera House and Gehry's gallery in Bilbao. If a society doesn't labor to be beautiful, it becomes indifferent to smog, litter, what Henry James called "trash triumphant," lurid communications, wretched TV, billboards, strip malls, blatancies of noise and confusion—or it considers these things the price you have to pay to make more money.

I have referred to "Adam's Curse" because my theme is the language of beauty: not beauty as such or a definition of the beautiful but beauty in its social manifestations, its discursive presence. Raymond Carver has a story, "What We Talk About When We Talk About Love." Replace love by beauty or "the beautiful," and you have a fair indication of my emphasis. I do not propose to be comprehensive: a few interventions will be, I hope, enough. But I should note, to begin with, that it is easy not to think about beauty or "the beautiful" or to talk about them. I spent many years in that condition without even knowing that it was a condition. I grew up in Warrenpoint, a small town in County Down, just across the border in Northern Ireland. It was not a town of much architectural or civic distinction, but its natural attributes were beautiful, placed as it was along the northern shore of Carlingford Loch, with Rostrevor, Kilkeel, and Newcastle on one side and, across the Loch, Omeath, Carlingford, and Greenore. Of these towns, Rostrevor was the most picturesque, mainly because it had the air of having till recently been a village, a charming open square in the center, and hilly streets leading to the Mourne mountains. The natural beauty of Warrenpoint was not enhanced by a shipyard, constructed during the World War II, and an industrial area in later years. Or by Newry, an ugly town five miles away. Still, a walk along the Shore Road from Warrenpoint to Rostrevor could have stirred my sense of beauty: mountains north and south, the Loch, and curve of the town as the Loch narrowed to become, after two or three miles, the Newry Canal.

I don't recall that I adverted to the beauty of those appearances. For me, Warrenpoint had social existence, classes and affiliations, but the question of its beauty did not arise. Even when I went to Dublin, as a student of Latin and English at University College, the question of beauty was not mentioned in class. We construed works of Shakespeare, Webster, Milton, Sir Thomas Browne, Virgil, Horace, Lucretius, Livy, and other writers, but even when we came to the extraordinary eloquence of Browne's *Hydriotaphia: Urn Burial,* our instructor did not help us to appreciate in any representative detail the beauty of the last chapter. During the same years I was also a student at the Royal Irish Academy of Music, concentrating on lieder with Brian Boydell as my teacher. He was a gifted man—composer, painter, singer, oboist, and conductor of the Dublin Orchestral Players. But he did not talk about beauty. I suppose his love of the music and his zeal in leading me through its difficulties implied the beauty he left otherwise to speak for itself. We studied mainly songs of Schubert, Schumann, Brahms—"Wie bist du meine Königen"—and Hugo Wolf, but we also spent many arduous weeks on Bach. The main problem was the frailty of my breathing, a defect especially drastic in attempting Bach's "Es ist Vollbracht" and, from Cantata 82, "Ich habe genug," which includes the most beautiful aria I had ever heard, "Schlummert ein." Now when I listen to Hans Hotter's recording of it, the music seems to sing itself. Hotter commits his feeling to its determination by the musical line; he never asserts himself or challenges the authority of the phrases. His interpretation consists of the tact with which he lets the first statement of the long descending line "fallet sanft und selig zu" govern the shape of the expression. Boydell tried hard to show me how to save my breath for the lines—

Welt, ich bleibe nicht mehr hier,

hab ich doch kein Teil an dir,

das der Seele könnte taugen—

—but I never reached "taugen" with more than a whisper left. Presumably Boydell decided that the beauty of the aria was best taken for granted and that I should submit myself to the phrasing of the lines without any expressive insistence.

If I did not think about beauty in those years, it follows that I never heard of its social and political implications. The people who ran art galleries and organized concerts in Dublin seemed to be mostly comfortable members of the middle class or upper middle class, so I was aware that in taking part in the musical life of the city I was rising above my origins. But that didn't trouble me, for the divisions of class were not severe. Or they could be mitigated by shared enthusiasms: music, painting, theater, sport. It did not occur to me that there was such a notion as "aesthetic ideology" or the idea that cultural achievements might be tools of the ruling class. I had not read Walter Benjamin's "Theses on the Philosophy of History" (1940), with its program for historical materialists:

> Whoever has emerged victorious participates to this day in the triumphal procession in which the present rulers step over those who are lying prostrate. According to traditional practice, the spoils are carried along in the procession. They are called cultural treasures, and a historical materialist views them with cautious detachment. For without exception the cultural treasures he surveys have an origin which he cannot contemplate without horror. They owe their existence not only to the efforts of the great minds and talents who have created them, but also to the anonymous toil of their contemporaries.

There is no document of civilization which is not at the same time a document of barbarism.[2]

I think I understand that assertion, but I don't know what to do with it. Granted that the Parthenon and the Egyptian pyramids were built by slaves who, most of them, did not survive to admire the fruits of their labor. I feel uneasy, perhaps even dispirited, by that reflection, but I can't feel guilty. I didn't whip those slaves into their compulsions. Nor can I regret that the Parthenon has at least in part survived. If there is a moral quandary here, I can't resolve it. Even in the small context of Dublin it did not occur to me that a painting in the National Gallery or someone's influence on the musical life of the city might be a sign of social or political authority and a means of maintaining it. In my little circle it wasn't. Brian Boydell was a distinguished presence, but he had no authority, power, or any evident desire to govern. His social class—Anglo-Irish Protestant, mercantile rather than aristocratic but bohemian in tone—was in decline, displaced by the new Catholic middle-class politicians who continue to run the country. Boydell had no power, only the prestige of being a musician and a colorful personage. I don't think he felt nostalgic for the centuries of Protestant Ascendancy or angry that the exercise of power in the land was likely to come into the hands of lower-middle-class Catholics like me. My relation to him was such that no question of aesthetic ideology or the guilt of cultural treasure arose.

If I ever thought of wider contexts, I did not know enough to suspect that a liberal society gets its way by making people feel that what they have to do coincides with what they want to do because it is accompanied by beautiful images. That notion was far beyond me. It was years before I read Benjamin's "Work of Art in the Age of Mechanical Reproduction" (1936) and its famous conclusion, which was not famous to me:

"Fiat ars—pereat mundus," says Fascism, and, as Marinetti admits, expects war to supply the artistic gratification of a sense perception that has been changed by technology. This is evidently the consummation of *"l'art pour l'art."* Mankind, which in Homer's time was an object of contemplation for the Olympian gods, now is one for itself. Its self-alienation has reached such a degree that it can experience its own destruction as an aesthetic pleasure of the first order. This is the situation of politics which Fascism is rendering aesthetic. Communism responds by politicizing art.[3]

The aestheticization of politics meant, then or later, Mussolini's march on Rome, the Nuremberg rallies, Leni Riefenstal's documentaries, the Olympic Games; but liberal democracy is also ready to recommend its war efforts by giving them an aesthetic form, as in films from *Mrs. Miniver* to *Saving Private Ryan.* The process was dramatically defined by Nietzsche and Wagner, despite their differences. Nietzsche's recommendation of the tragic hero confronting the pain of death presented an image of the beautiful in far more compelling terms than any otherwise available felicities. Wagner endowed the sentiment of the nation with mythic grandeur and beauty as the histrionic form of spirit, claiming to express not this individual life or that but life as such, the essence of it.

These notions are contentious, or have been, mainly because they soon become moral and ethical issues. For several years, especially after 1968, you were thought to be a boor if, reading *Mansfield Park,* you were not beset with wondering what Sir Thomas's business interests in Antigua were and whether they entailed slave-driving.[4] But it is my impression that the "politicization" of literary studies has receded somewhat in the past few years. "Theory" is no longer the punitive discourse it was when Michel Foucault, Jacques Derrida, Paul de Man, Stanley Fish, Fredric Jameson, and their colleagues were first engaged in it. The tone of "cultural studies" is not now as acrimonious as it has been. Scholars who write about gender, race, and sexual disposition—in their bearing on the writing and reading of literature—have found readers to follow the arguments, but these readers have settled into constituencies (journals, conferences, seminars) which don't demand that everyone pay attention. Most of the disputes are between one feminist and another: outsiders do not feel implicated. "Post-colonial" scholars have to learn what to think not just about *A Passage to India* and *Burger's Daughter* but about globalization and how it differs from the older forms of empire. It may be, too, that the leading figures in the culture wars have had their say and retired from the field. Some of them have taken up other issues or lost faith in their causes. But, for whatever reason, there is more space for themes—beauty is one of them—which not long ago were held to be regressive. The word "aesthetic" is no longer a term of abuse and contempt. In *Words Alone: The Poet T. S. Eliot* (2000), I referred to Irving Howe and the discrepancy, as it appeared to him, between his Socialism and the pleasure he took in Balanchine's ballets as danced by the New York City Ballet. He felt that he had to explain himself. He imagined Tolstoy denouncing him for reveling in Suzanne Farrell's and Peter Martins's dancing of *Chaconne*. But in the end Howe thought of telling Tolstoy that "there are kinds of beauty before which the moral imagination ought to withdraw, and that in my lifetime these kinds of beauty have been served well by Balanchine."[5] He did not explain how or why these kinds of beauty were exempted from moral rebuke. Howe published *A Margin of Hope* in 1982. I don't think he would feel obliged, if he were writing now, to justify the beauty he saw in *Chaconne* or his frequent attendance at Lincoln Center.

Another sign of this mellowness in recent intellectual weather is the concessiveness apparent in a good deal of contemporary scholarship, the decision freely arrived at not always to insist. In a recent essay welcoming the "return of the beautiful," Alexander Nehamas says that "beauty is not a determinate feature of things (as the dismal failure of all attempts to define it implies)." I'm not sure that he's right. Irving Howe, Richard Poirier, Robert Garis, and a few other critics could say, with fair persuasiveness, why *Chaconne* or *Robert Schumann's Davidsbundlertanze* is beautiful. What they could not do is show that the qualities of those ballets are present in every work or object which is claimed to be beautiful. But that doesn't seem a disqualification. We can manage reasonably well by saying what is beautiful in such-and-such without feeling bound to attempt a comprehensive definition of beauty. Nehamas says that the merit of beauty is that "its value is always in question." Presumably he means that the questioning discourse is valuable in itself, though he doesn't say why it is good to keep questioning rather than to reach an answer. Further, he maintains:

> Kant said that the judgment of taste is not "based on concepts." By that he meant that no description, however detailed, could ever prove that something is beautiful (unless it has already smuggled in a reference to beauty): "There can be no rule according to which anyone is to be forced to recognize anything as beautiful." He was right, but not for the reasons he gave. He was right because judgment does not come at the end of our interaction with beautiful things. It is not a report on their features or the feelings they have provoked. The judgment of

beauty is not a conclusion that cannot be justified, but a guess that might be wrong. It is an intimation that what stands before us is valuable in ways we do not yet understand, but that intimation might be profoundly misleading. We find things beautiful—in nature, in people, in art—when we sense we have not exhausted them, and our eyes, as Nietzsche wrote specifically about artists, "remain fixed on what remains veiled, even after the unveiling." Beautiful things are those we still desire, in every sense, to possess and know better. The perception of beauty is inseparable from yearning.[6]

This is alien to Kant. Kant would regard the desire to possess the beautiful thing, in any sense, as disabling to the aesthetic experience. He did not include endlessly postponed yearning among the attributes of an aesthetic experience. I. A. Richards's claim that a work of art is "inexhaustible to meditation" is nearer the Kantian mark, because meditation isn't possession or desire; it leaves the work of art available to other people. But Nehamas's move from "judgment" to "guess" is an example of the concessiveness I've mentioned. I take it he means an educated guess, not that anything goes. The one who guesses would like to persuade other people that the guess is convincing.

There is still the question of taste. I recall being bewildered, in Dublin, when I came across T. S. Eliot's assertion that criticism "must always profess an end in view, which, roughly speaking, appears to be the elucidation of works of art and the correction of taste."[7] Elucidation, yes, which includes "putting the reader in possession of facts which he would otherwise have missed":[8] that and so much more. But I did not know what taste was, how it could be—Eliot used these words—"vicious" or "corrupt," or if it was, how it could be corrected. I assume that taste is a just pleasure, commensurate with the object that provokes it: my taste is vicious or corrupt if the object in view is not worth thinking of or should not have provoked my liking at all. My general admiration of Dave Hickey is qualified by his preferring Norman Rockwell to Picasso and Cézanne. I was appalled when I heard Sir William Walton, in a BBC television interview, disparaging Mahler. It would be heavy work to show Hickey or Walton why he should reconsider his likes and dislikes, but I suppose it could be done and that critics should try to foster good taste rather than bad. Tastes differ, but critics should not relax on that consideration.

We have evidence, then, that beauty is discussible. We hear that it is "back." But it would not be an entirely happy experience to discover that it has settled down among the standard values and that it is no longer a difficult issue. That would mean that society has assimilated yet another value to its own purposes. Beauty, whether we try to define it or not, should maintain its recalcitrance and go its own way. I think of two stories by Hawthorne as parables of this determination. In the first, we are to think of beauty and the rough conditions it has to meet in the world; in the second, of the exorbitance to which a certain kind of person is driven in the attempt to secure it.

In "The Artist of the Beautiful" (1844) Hawthorne tells of Owen Warland, a young man who works as a watch-repairer but who lives his true life in search of the beautiful. He is gifted with an acute sense of the delicate and the minute. Mind and hand are turned toward the exquisite. Owen thinks of his work as a tribute to Annie Hovenden, whom he loves and regards as his ideal companion, best recipient of the beautiful. For her he makes a metal butterfly that perches on one's hand, flies off, and returns. It is a work of extraordinary refinement. But Annie marries Robert Danforth, the local blacksmith, a man of iron, and they have a child who resembles his father in that respect. Annie's father, Peter Hovenden, was once a watchmaker and Owen's master, but he is now retired. He is a materialist and despises Owen's yearning for the exquisite. The story turns upon some of Hawthorne's favorite polarities: light and dark, gold and iron, spirit and body, the beautiful and the useful. The implied narrator is on Owen's side, because he believes that the "deeds of earth, however etherealized by piety or genius, are without value, except as exercises and manifestations of the spirit." Owen strives "to put the very spirit of beauty into form and give it motion." After many tribulations and lapses during which he ceases "to be an inhabitant of the better sphere that lies unseen around us," he succeeds in making the butterfly, giving it his own life. One evening he shows it to Annie, Robert, their child, and Peter:

> Nature's ideal butterfly was here realized in all its perfection; not in the pattern of such faded insects as flit among earthly flowers, but of those which hover across the meads of paradise for child-angels and the spirits of departed infants to disport themselves with. The rich down was visible upon its wings; the luster of its eyes seemed instinct with spirit. The firelight glimmered around this wonder—the candles gleamed upon it; but it glistened apparently by its own radiance, and illuminated the finger and outstretched hand on which it rested with a white gleam like that of precious stones. In its perfect beauty, the consideration of size was entirely lost. Had its wings overreached the firmament, the mind could not have been more filled or satisfied.[9]

Annie thinks it beautiful and wants to know if is it alive. Robert laughs at it. Peter wants only to see how it works. The child grabs it. In a few moments, meeting these roughnesses and vulgarities, the butterfly loses its beauty and dies. "In an atmosphere of doubt and mockery," as Owen says, "its exquisite susceptibility suffers torture, as does the soul of him who instilled his own life into it." The narrator reports:

> The blacksmith, by main force, unclosed the infant's hand, and found within the palm a small heap of glittering fragments, whence the mystery of beauty had fled forever. And as for Owen Warland, he looked placidly at what seemed the ruin of his life's labor, and which was yet no ruin. He had caught a far other butterfly than this. When the artist rose high enough to achieve the beautiful, the symbol by which he made it perceptible to mortal senses became of little value in his eyes while his spirit possessed itself in the enjoyment of the Reality.[10]

"He had caught a far other butterfly than this." Hawthorne imagines that the artist of the beautiful copes with the Platonic discrepancy between the Idea and its embodiments, or between spirit and matter, precisely by not seeking to reconcile them. He comes to realize that the Reality is spirit. The narrator grieves that the artist must consume his life trying for a reconciliation, a fulfillment of opposites:

> Alas, that the artist, whether in poetry or whatever other material, may not content himself with the inward enjoyment of the Beautiful, but must chase the flitting mystery beyond the verge of his ethereal domain, and crush its frail being in seizing it with a material grasp! Owen Warland felt the impulse to give external reality to his ideas, as irresistibly as any

of the poets or painters, who have arrayed the world in a dimmer and fainter beauty, imperfectly copied from the richness of their visions.[11]

According to the rhetoric of the story, the only thing that matters is that Owen has had his vision of beauty. The butterfly, the composed object, the imperfect copy, does not count for much in that comparison. Owen can look placidly at the thing he has made, even when the grubby child has destroyed it, because it is at one remove from the vision he has had. It may trouble him that the representative people of the world have no sense of its beauty, but—no matter—he has had his vision, and it is irrefutable. A definition is not required. It would be agreeable if Annie had appreciated Owen as the supreme artist of the beautiful and kept herself free of the blacksmith's attentions, but that, too, doesn't matter much in the end. The crucial event is Owen's relation to the vision of beauty he has had.

The moral of "The Birthmark" is different. Aylmer, a man of science, marries Georgiana, a woman beautiful in every respect except for a birthmark in the shape of a hand on her left cheek. Many people have called the birthmark a charm, but Aylmer longs to see it removed. It is to him the "visible mark of earthly imperfection":

It was the fatal flaw of humanity which Nature, in one shape or another, stamps ineffaceably on all her productions, either to imply that they are temporary and finite, or that their perfection must be wrought by toil and pain. The crimson hand expressed the ineludible gripe in which mortality clutches the highest and purest of earthly mould, degrading them into kindred with the lowest, and even with the very brutes, like whom their visible frames return to dust. In this manner, selecting it as the symbol of his wife's liability to sin, sorrow, decay, and death, Aylmer's somber imagination was not long in rendering the birthmark a frightful object, causing him more trouble and horror than ever Georgiana's beauty, whether of soul or sense, had given him delight.[12]

Georgiana proposes that Aylmer employ his skill to remove the birthmark, at whatever risk and cost to her, "for life, while this hateful mark makes me the object of your horror and disgust,— life is a burden which I would fling down with joy." Aylmer is convinced that he can remove the blemish:

> "I feel myself fully competent to render this dear cheek as faultless as its fellow; and then, most beloved, what will be my triumph when I shall have corrected what Nature left imperfect in her fairest work! Even Pygmalion, when his sculptured woman assumed life, felt not greater ecstasy than mine will be."[13]

Georgiana tells him to proceed, even though "you should find the birthmark take refuge in my heart at last." She thinks it a proof of his love, "so pure and lofty that it would accept nothing less than perfection nor miserably make itself contented with an earthlier nature than he had dreamed of." She feels "how much more precious was such a sentiment than that meaner kind which would have borne with the imperfection for her sake, and have been guilty of treason to holy love by degrading its perfect idea to the level of the actual." Aylmer concocts a liquor which he thinks can't fail to remove the birthmark. Georgiana drinks it and falls asleep. The birthmark begins to recede. Georgiana awakes, sees her cleared cheek, but feels herself dying:

"My poor Aylmer," she repeated, with a more than human tenderness, "you have aimed loftily; you have done nobly. Do not repent that with so high and pure a feeling, you have rejected the best the earth could offer. Aylmer, dearest Aylmer, I am dying!"[14]

The birthmark, the "fatal hand," had grappled with the mystery of life, "and was the bond by which an angelic spirit kept itself in union with a mortal frame":

As the last crimson tint of the birthmark—that sole token of human imperfection—faded from her cheek, the parting breath of the now perfect woman passed into the atmosphere, and her soul, lingering a moment near her husband, took its heavenward flight. Then a hoarse, chuckling laugh was heard again! Thus ever does the gross fatality of earth exult in its invariable triumph over the immortal essence which, in this dim sphere of half development, demands the completeness of a higher state. Yet, had Aylmer reached a profounder wisdom, he need not thus have flung away the happiness which would have woven his mortal life of the selfsame texture with the celestial. The momentary circumstance was too strong for him; he failed to look beyond the shadowy scope of time, and, living once for all in eternity, to find the perfect future in the present.[15]

The laugh comes from Aminadab, Aylmer's servant, a man of earth who was "incapable of comprehending a single principle" but well able to execute the details of Aylmer's experiments. But it was Aminadab who represented, earlier in the story, the acceptance of whatever is given and in the best possible mode: "If she were my wife, I'd never part with that birthmark," he said to himself. For the moment, matter is wiser than spirit, and more humane.

What "The Birthmark" implies is not merely that the search for perfect beauty in this world is vain or that the body—Georgiana's—on which the scientist foists his desire for perfection wishes to die rather than remain blemished; but that it is a mark of the profounder wisdom to see the imperfect as our paradise, the perfect future as the present. According to "The Artist of the Beautiful," beauty lives in Owen's vision and nowhere else: its partial manifestations are secondary. According to "The Birthmark," beauty thrives in what the one-eyed man sees as imperfection. The only way to reconcile the two stories is to construe "the present" as not merely the circumstances we happen to be given but the vision of beauty we can rise to in that limited dimension.

A philosophic definition of beauty is not needed here. Even without it, the word "beauty" can be used in sentences, and it can be significantly accompanied. In the eighth chapter of *Ulysses* Leopold Bloom has been enjoying a light lunch—a cheese sandwich and a glass of Burgundy—in Davy Byrne's public house and admiring the oak bar-counter: "Nice piece of wood in that counter. Nicely planed. Like the way it curves there." One curve suggests other curves, and Bloom recalls Molly, screened under ferns on the Hill of Howth, giving him her breasts, "woman's breasts full in her blouse of nun's veiling, fat nipples upright." Looking back at the bar: "His downcast eyes followed the silent veining of the oaken slab. Beauty: it curves: curves are beauty. Shapely goddesses, Venus, Juno: curves the world admires." [16] You can surround the word with companions and let the spaces between them hold it sufficiently in place. In *Mrs. Dalloway* Clarissa stumbles into reminding Peter Walsh that he had wanted to marry her: "Of course I did, thought

Peter; it almost broke my heart too, he thought; and was overcome with his own grief, which rose like a moon looked at from
a terrace, ghastly beautiful with light from the sunken day."[17] If
"beautiful" were by itself in that sentence, it could not do much
work, but it is lit by "ghastly" and even more luridly by "sunken,"
and in that double light we sense what it means for the moon to
appear ghastly beautiful to someone in grief.

Leopold Bloom is a lay aesthetician, and that only as occasion
prompts him. "The silent veining of the oaken slab" may be a
narrative perception, not his. He starts perceiving again when he
thinks of beauty and curves. He is not anticipating an argument
between those who admire the curves of Henry Moore's sculptures or Brancusi's more than the straight lines of Donald Judd's.
Bloom's aesthetics is local and opportunistic. This applies, too,
to most of us. In well-off societies we say of Moore, Brancusi,
and Judd: let us have them all, we can afford them. As for beauty,
we adopt as fashions for the moment whatever we happen to like
of other cultures, especially of those we want to patronize. Some
women cultivate an impression of elongated necks by wearing
forty or more rings under their uplifted chins: the practice is
exotic in the West, being of African provenance, but Imam has
given it her authority on the runway, she has made it beautiful.
No cultural issue arises. Our cultural practices are anthologies,
and from time to time we bring out revised editions. We think
some appearances beautiful, or we do not. We rarely ask why an
artifact is looked at in that way. Is beauty an intrinsic value, a
good in itself, which can be associated with other values — social, religious, sexual, commercial? Is it self-evident that beautiful appearances are to be regarded intrinsically? I have not seen
any attempt to consider a question that T. S. Eliot raised in a
review of two books by W. J. Perry, *The Growth of Civilisation*
and *The Origin of Magic and Religion:*

The arts developed incidentally to the search for objects of talismanic properties. The Egyptian who first fashioned gold into a likeness of a cowrie-shell, the Cretan who designed an octopus on his pottery, the Indian who hung a necklace of bear's-teeth about his neck, were not aiming primarily at decoration, but invoking the assistance of life-giving amulets. At what point, may we ask, does the attempt to design and create an object for the sake of beauty become conscious? At what point in civilization does any conscious distinction between practical or magical utility and aesthetic beauty arise? These questions are not asked or answered by Mr. Perry. But surely the distinction must mark a change in the human mind which is of fundamental importance. And a further question we should be impelled to ask is this: Is it possible and justifiable for art, the creation of beautiful objects and of literature, to persist indefinitely without its primitive purposes: is it possible for the aesthetic object to be a *direct* object of attention?[18]

Clearly it is possible. But Eliot is raising a harder question: is the production of beautiful objects which have no relation to "the search for objects of talismanic properties" axiomatically justifiable? If you walk through the Museum of Modern Art in New York and look at one perhaps beautiful object after another, you may find the profusion gorgeous and think it self-justified. Or you may reflect, as Eliot did, on communities in which works of art were fewer but each of them was validated as a life-giving amulet. If you want to see talismanic beauty you must go into the churches and look at the priestly vestments on days of festival, or into museums of ancient art, or to any of the few communities in which such a value is perpetuated. In other places, the "culture industry," as Adorno called it, has taken command. Since the eighteenth century we have assumed that the profusion of intrinsically beautiful objects without any relation to a deeper cultural practice is justifiable, and that the beauty of an object is all the more precious for being free of social function. Kant was the aesthetician of this conviction, especially when art was seen as subordinate to the aesthetic value of the natural world. In the meantime, the commercialization of art has removed its intrinsic or useless quality and turned the beautiful object into common processes of exchange.

I

Speaking of Beauty

I

A short list of values would include these: life, love, truth, virtue, justice, and beauty. To these might be added: power, belief, communication, and money. There might be disputes about one or another of these, but I think there would be fairly wide agreement about the list. Disagreements would arise about the relative status of each value, and about the impingement of one value on other ones, but these issues could be resolved with time and goodwill. I'm not sure how to resolve the problem that each value, once acknowledged, tends to take over the world in its favor and to jostle its rivals aside. Values do not divide the world of experience into separate domains and keep the peace among them, each staying within its proper space. When you pay attention to a particular value, it seems to extend its purview, so that in the end nothing seems to be beyond its reach. I think of Peter Walsh in *Mrs. Dalloway* getting ready to go to Clarissa's party. His mood is such that beauty, after an initial trembling, seems to be everywhere: there is no point at which it desists or yields to other considerations. He believes that he is about to have an experience. But of what?

> Beauty anyhow. Not the crude beauty of the eye.
> It was not beauty pure and simple—Bedford Place
> leading into Russell Square. It was straightness and
> emptiness of course; the symmetry of a corridor;
> but it was also windows lit up, a piano, a gramo-
> phone sounding; a sense of pleasure-making hid-

den, but now and again emerging when, through the uncurtained window, the window left open, one saw parties sitting over tables, young people slowly circling, conversations between men and women, maids idly looking out (a strange comment theirs, when work was done), stockings drying on top ledges, a parrot, a few plants. Absorbing, mysterious, of infinite richness, this life. And in the large square where the cabs shot and swerved so quick, there were loitering couples, dallying, embracing, shrunk up under the shower of a tree; that was moving; so silent, so absorbed, that one passed, discreetly, timidly, as if in the presence of some sacred ceremony to interrupt which would have been impious. That was interesting. And so on into the flare and glare.[1]

Several disciplines might stake a claim to those little episodes: the politics of cities, the sociology of class—those maids, those cab drivers, the disposition of work and entertainment—and the psychology of flare and glare. But Virginia Woolf lets Peter Walsh enjoy the privilege of beauty, such that no other value is allowed to take over the occasion. For the time being, Peter is an aesthete, and the social appearances pass before his eyes without asking to be otherwise judged. He is indiscriminate, seeing what he sees. He has come back from India for business and a little pleasure. In an hour or two he will make his way to Clarissa Dalloway's party, and other values will intrude, but for the moment, the beauty of London on an evening in June folds every appearance in its embrace. Or rather: Peter's sense of beauty looks for gratification, and finds it. I leave aside the question: are these sentiments plausibly Peter's, or is the narration, the style, perceiving for him in ways he would hardly be able to rise to?

We are encouraged to think that his sense of beauty is at least of the same order as the one we find in Woolf's sentences, if a little short of it in degree.

In what follows I have little to say about beauty, and I say most of that little indirectly or by the way. I don't claim that my sense of beauty differs much from anyone else's who lives in the West, or that it settles upon special instances. If someone remarks that Julia Roberts and Jennifer Lopez are beautiful, I find no cause to disagree. My theme is not beauty but how we talk about it; how they, you, and I talk about it, and why we say the things we say. Not surprisingly, the book is rife with quotations. I wish there were more of them and that everything I say in my own behalf could be given in footnotes.

It is not clear why we talk about beauty at all unless we have nothing else to talk about. It is surprising to hear it referred to in important contexts, as in William Empson's claims that the "prime intellectual difficulty of our age is that true beliefs may make it impossible to act rightly; that we cannot think without verbal fictions; that they must not be taken for true beliefs, and yet must be taken seriously; that it is essential to analyse beauty; essential to accept it unanalysed; essential to believe that the universe is deterministic; essential to act as if it was not."[2] I agree with the claims about beauty, and the necessity of verbal fictions, while the other ones seem to me disputable at best. But the most surprisingly edifying thing is that the question of beauty is raised along with questions of truth, belief, fiction, moral action, and the nature of the universe.

I'll postpone more difficult considerations of beauty and start with a few relatively straightforward points. Why should we regard the beauty of a beautiful thing? (1) Because its existence is analogous to—not the same as—the good and the true it once symbolized. That's a decent reason. I'll come back to it. (2) Because looking at a beautiful thing for its beauty fosters in us certain intuitions that other forces in life have no time for— respect for intrinsic value, freedom, independence, selflessness. That reason is according to Kant, and I think well of it, but it would be hard to protect it against the intrusions of a pornographer. (3) Because it encourages a contemplative, appreciative, patient attitude in us and at least rebukes automatic recourse to appetitive desires. That's much the same as the Kantian reason, but it lays claim to a slightly different range of feelings. It's also at one with Novalis's claim that the beautiful always appears to be so much at rest: "Everything beautiful is a *self-illuminated*, *perfect individual*."[3] (4) Because "the appreciation of beauty in art or nature is not only (for all its difficulties) the easiest available spiritual exercise; it is also a completely adequate entry into (and not just analogy of) the good life, since it *is* the checking of selfishness in the interest of seeing the real."[4] That reason is Iris Murdoch's. I wonder what she means by "spiritual" and by her appeal to "the good life" and the beautiful as a means of entry to it; but the point about checking selfishness and seeing the real strengthens the case. (5) Because a beautiful thing holds its own and remains unintimidated by the analytic zeal that Hegel ascribes to the Understanding. That reason is my own, only so far as I have deduced it from an opaque paragraph in *Phenomenology of Spirit*. Hegel appears to say that it is the work of the Understanding to analyze an idea—that is, to bring to bear upon it the power of the negative, to rid the idea of the form in which it has become familiar. "Beauty, powerless and helpless, hates understanding, because the latter exacts from it what it cannot perform."[5] I think this means that beauty cannot deconstruct itself, cannot have itself broken into its elements or allow its forms to become "a possession of pure self-consciousness."[6] The beautiful thing holds its secret by allowing us to divine that it has one. I see no reason why it should yield to the analytic pressure of the

Understanding: each has its own privileged way of acting in the world.

A theory of beauty would be a good thing to have, if it could be secured without ideological insistence. It is more urgent to have a theory of truth or, better still, a principle of truth, so that we can decide whether a particular statement should count as true or false. A president of the United States was nearly impeached because he said, on national television, "I did not have sexual relations with that woman." True or false? And if false, what should follow? A principle of justice is necessary if we are to decide whether a certain act is reprehensible. Discussions of these issues are likely to be difficult, and perhaps interminable, as Alasdair MacIntyre maintains in *After Virtue*, because there is no common ground of values, and our moral vocabularies are mere shards from systems of values no longer in force. Some philosophers hold to a theory of truth as the demonstrable correspondence of a statement to the irresistible facts of the case, while others insist on pragmatic usefulness, contingency, or the social construction of truth. Scholars of justice may think that justice is a value dependent on one's informed conscience or on a social contract, a consideration of someone's need, or a consequence of Natural Law. At least we know what the main issues are, if not how to reach agreement on war, "crimes against humanity," abortion, or the death penalty. And yet we continue to say without much hesitation that such-and-such and so-and-so are beautiful: tulips, roses, certain women, certain men, most children, a page of Chinese written characters, an African mask, a mathematical process, a piece of music, the view from Portofino, a certain sunset, a full moon, some animals (but not the rhinoceros), kingfishers, dragonflies, the air at Brighton, Alexander Kipnis's voice, the weather when noon's a purple glow. These, we say, are beautiful, but we let our appreciation rest on the adjective, we don't say what makes them beautiful or justifies a claim that they are: we don't feel a need to go questing from adjective to noun.

Granted that the true and the good are more urgent considerations than the beautiful, we may doubt the merit of keeping the three of them separate. Meanwhile, to be specific: suppose you were walking with a friend in the Louvre, hovering to look at this Ghirlandaio, that Giorgione, that Correggio, murmuring "beautiful, beautiful" or other words to that effect: ah, gosh, gorgeous, ravishing, exquisite. It would be tiresome if your friend interrupted your gaze on Mantegna's *Calvary* to ask: "Yes, but what do you mean by beautiful?" You might try saying several things. The painting thrills me. It must illuminate my life. It provokes in me a semblance of desire, virtual rather than appetitive. It is beautiful to see such agony brought to performance and composition. The painting helps me to imagine what it would be to be crucified. The beauty of the painting gives a conviction of life, death, and redemption to what is otherwise a mere story about Christ and two thieves. Look at the bald soldier, returned to his own business. The painting shows the horror composed in form as it could not be composed otherwise in life. It is something understood. These would not be foolish statements, but they would not lead to further or more clarifying conversation. The talk would have to move to a different tone, another topic, which suggests that such words as "beautiful" or "ravishing" belong to the structure of social amenities and are not expected to do much work in cognition or elucidation. They merely indicate that a conversation is going on.

The most immediate reason to talk about beauty is the hope of saving it from the mercenary embrace of TV and advertisements. The hope is a frail one, since the owners of these instruments make their money by effecting strong links of association between health, beauty, high spirits, and sex. They are not interested in a theory of beauty, unless such a theory proves necessary to keep the links of desirable associations in place. There is no sign of that. The associations are mutually and reliably sustaining. So a theory of beauty, or talk of beauty, is likely to be sought only by people who want to round out their informal exclamations—"beautiful, beautiful"—by giving them a larger and more thoughtful context of speech. Schiller had this in view in the sixteenth letter on the aesthetic education of mankind, where he distinguished between the "man of action" and the "reflective man":

> The reflective man conceives of virtue, truth, happiness; but the man of action will only exercise virtues, only apprehend truths, only enjoy happy days. To lead back these latter to the former—to achieve instead of moral practices, morality, instead of things known, knowledge, instead of happy experiences, happiness, is the business of physical and ethical education; to make Beauty from beautiful objects is the task of aesthetic education.[7]

This is a worthy aim, if only because it would add to the number of occasions on which we know what we are talking about. But there are special problems when the theme is beauty.

One of them is the general decline in the use (except for professional purposes of law and the courts) of abstractions or "terms of concept," as Josephine Miles calls them. In the literature of the sixteenth and seventeenth centuries it was common to invoke such terms as goodness, truth, and beauty without even having to personify them: they exerted their force as values simply by being named. As in Donne's "Communitie":

> Good we must love, and must hate ill,
> For ill is ill and good, good still.[8]

Miles has pointed out that "beauty" persisted through the eighteenth and nineteenth centuries in a vocabulary involving "the love of the God of nature":

> It was the Protestant belief that the goodness of God expressed itself especially through the world of nature, through mountains, seas, skies, receivable as images directly through man's senses and therefore an aesthetic as well as an ethical message. Protestants scorned the intrusive human endeavor in the art of stained glass in church windows, for example; they wanted their windows to be pure clear glass to reveal the aesthetic sensory truth of the universe outside. Though the triad of values including beauty had been familiar since Plato, increasingly the scenes and shapes and colors of nature had something to do with God's meaning for man, and words like *light* and *dark, green* and *golden* in their abundance supported the sensory meaning of beauty. So *good* and *true* began to be subordinated.[9]

Since the nineteenth century, in literature as in conversation, the terms of concept have faded. It is unusual to find a modern poet, as here James Merrill, writing—

> Some who have perfect beauty do not grieve,
> As I, when beauty passes. They've known merit
> In word, emotion, deed:
> Lone angels round each human grave . . .[10]

—and even in that case Merrill had to support his abstractions with four earlier stanzas describing one version of beauty, the peacock's, and to establish a curial style in which appeals to moral or aesthetic abstractions would not break the decorum. More often, beauty as a term of concept has been replaced by "the language of bodies and houses as it adapts itself to the tradition of concepts, scenes, feelings, and objects." Beautiful things, in modern poetry, are rarely called beautiful, but, as Miles says, "they are shown to be so by the constructed centers of care in which they are presented."[11]

There is also a question of the social classes and the different delicacies of conversation they feature. In some countries and among certain classes, talk of beauty is regarded as shocking unless the speaker is homosexual: then concessions are made. In heterosexual society, references to beauty are rare. Only the succulence of a hot gammon makes it plausible, in "The Waste Land," for Lil and Albert to ask their garrulous friend in to dinner "to get the beauty of it hot."[12] B. H. Fairchild's poem "Beauty" starts with a man and his wife, tourists in Florence, looking at Donatello's "David" in the Bargello museum:

> We are at the Bargello in Florence, and she says,
> *What are you thinking?* And I say, *Beauty*, thinking
> of how very far we are now from the machine shop
> and the dry fields of Kansas, the treeless horizons
> of slate skies and the muted passions of roughnecks
> and scrabble farmers drunk and romantic enough
> to weep more or less silently at the darkened end
> of the bar out of, what else, loneliness, meaning
> the ache of thwarted desire, of, in a word, *beauty*,
> or rather its absence, and it occurs to me again
> that no male member of my family has ever used
> this word in my hearing or anyone else's except
> in reference, perhaps, to a new pickup or dead deer.
> *By God, Henry, that's a beauty.*[13]

Fairchild's speaker—we may call him Fairchild, the poem being clearly autobiographical—is probably not thinking, there in the

Bargello, about beauty but wondering why the "David" is so beautiful. Saying "Beauty" to his wife makes the conversation formal, seriously discursive: it is not a time for trivia. Then the discrepancy strikes him between looking at the beautiful bronze and being back in Kansas. He recalls, as a boy in 1963, watching television and being astonished to see Robert Penn Warren and Paul Weiss talking about beauty:

> Here were two grown men discussing beauty
> seriously and with dignity as if they and the topic
> were as normal as normal topics of discussion
> between men, such as soybean prices or why
> the commodities market was a sucker's game
> or Oklahoma football or Gimpy Neiderland
> almost dying from his hemorrhoid operation.
> They were discussing beauty and tossing around
> allusions to Plato and Aristotle and someone
> named Pater, and they might be homosexuals.[14]

Other memories: Fairchild's Uncle Ross from California calling his mother's Sunday dinner centerpiece "lovely" and his father leaving the room in embarrassment; the assassination of President Kennedy and the Zapruder film shown repeatedly on television, and Fairchild and his pals sitting around in the machine shop—

> staring at the tin ceiling like a giant screen,
> *What a strange goddamned country,* as Bobby Sudduth
> arches a wadded Fritos bag at the time clock and says,
> *Oswald, from that far, you got to admit, that shot was a*
> *beauty.*[15]

—two workers from California stripping off their clothes in the middle of the shop; Bobby Sudduth killing himself with a single shot of a twelve gauge. The poem ends with Fairchild and his wife still in the Bargello:

> *What are you thinking?* She asks again, and so I begin
> to tell her about a strange afternoon in Kansas,
> about something I have never spoken of, and we walk
> to a window where the shifting light spreads a sheen
> along the casement, and looking out, we see the city
> blazing like miles of uncut wheat, the farthest buildings
> taken in their turn, and the great dome, the way
> the metal roof of the machine shop, I tell her,
> would break into flame late on an autumn day, with such
> beauty.[16]

Kansas can't be the only place in which a heterosexual man never uses the word "beauty" except to refer to a dead deer, a new pickup, or Lee Harvey Oswald's prowess with a rifle. Or where a young man needs to go to Florence in the equal company of his wife and stand with her to look at Donatello's "David" before he can surmount the inhibition preventing him from talking about beautiful things. Still, it is an achievement to note the shifting light spreading a sheen along the casement in the gallery, and to compare Florence to "miles of uncut wheat," the comparison honoring both parts of it and the sun that shines impartially on each. The abstract word "beauty" has made such aesthetic precision feasible.

Even in polite society, beauty is difficult to talk about, if only because the words nearest to it are gestures, though not necessarily empty ones. "It is a beauteous evening, calm and free." Of Wordsworth's three adjectives, only one is doing any work. We know what a calm evening is like, and being out and about in it may make one feel free, but we don't know what makes an evening beauteous. In the lines that follow, beauteous and free are not further clarified; they yield at once to intimations of a religious, worshipful scene in which the need for clarification is sublimed away. No prosaic requirement asserts itself in lines hushed by these words and phrases: holy, nun, adoration, heaven, eternal, divine, "in Abraham's bosom," worship'st, Temple, shrine, and ultimately "God being with thee when we know it not."[17] Wordsworth is not using "beauteous" and "free" irresponsibly: he is relying on the spiritual implications of the later words to fulfill the latency of the earlier ones by drawing them into a context which they have hardly as much as adumbrated.

In an essay on Shakespeare's "The Phoenix and Turtle," Barbara Everett calls the poem "brilliant and beautiful," and she refers to "the surreal (and very beautiful, if sometimes almost mocking) intellectuality of the middle stanzas." The poem is a "Renaissance jewel, beautiful but (compared to *Hamlet*) troublingly unvoiced, relatively toneless, unchangeably small." She speaks again of the "arcanely beautiful court dialect of love" in the poem and, comparing it with the songs in Sidney's *Astrophel and Stella,* names the eighth of these, the one that begins "In a grove most rich of shade," as "the most beautiful of them."[18] "Beautiful" in Everett's sentences is not a word of description or designation, nor is it an empty gesture; it is a tribute, a smile, a celebration that leaves to other words the pleasure of saying more precisely what is being celebrated. She doesn't try to make "beautiful" touch upon the reasons she has for thinking the poem beautiful. This may be warranted by the poem itself, which ends with four stanzas of lament, the first of which takes it for granted that the values it honors are absolute, such that they require no adjectives or further reasons in their favor:

> Beauty, truth, and rarity,
> Grace in all simplicity,
> Here enclos'd in cinders lie.[19]

Five terms of concept are gathered by the emphatic "Here" to lie not destroyed in cinders but enclosed in them: their values don't need to be protected, but they are.

In an essay on A. E. Housman, Anthony Lane tries to keep the word "beauty" close to the reasons he has for invoking it. He quotes the second and third stanzas of Housman's "Tell me not here, it needs not saying":

> On russet floors, by waters idle,
>   The pine lets fall its cone;
> The cuckoo shouts all day at nothing
>   In leafy dells alone;
> And traveller's joy beguiles in autumn
>   Hearts that have lost their own.
>
> On acres of the seeded grasses
>   The changing burnish heaves;
> Or marshalled under moons of harvest
>   Stand still all night the sheaves;
> Or beaches strip in storms for winter
>   And stain the wind with leaves.[20]

Lane remarks of these stanzas that "sometimes a single word is enough to crack the mood, and to rescue the beautiful from the menace of the pretty." "Shouts, heaves, strip, stain: this was not a writer who turned up his nose or averted his gaze."[21] Lane evidently assumes that "the pretty" is a menace, a temptation—it gives itself to us when our attention is distracted—and that we achieve "the beautiful" by rejecting these blandishments. Leafy dells are pretty, and pretty cheap, but shouts, heaves, strip, and stain are more demanding, and yield beauty in the end. It is daring to have the beaches actively stripping—like an athlete stripping down—for winter, when a second thought would see them stripped by the storms. The verbs that Lane doesn't mention—"lets fall," "beguiles," "have lost," and "stand"—are presumably not stern enough. The difference between beautiful and pretty is that you have to keep your nose to the ground and your gaze concentrated to achieve one but not the other. In the days of the New Criticism this degree of attention was called not beauty but irony: the quality was enough to distinguish good poets from bad, because good poets did not allow themselves to be beguiled by poetic diction to the extent of pretending that other factors, recalcitrant and prosaic, were not in the scene. Robert Penn Warren's preference for impure rather than pure poetry made the same claim as Cleanth Brooks's "Irony as a Principle of Structure." Bad poets could not run the risk of seeing awkward things that good poets insisted on seeing. But neither Brooks nor Warren produced any good reason for thinking that irony and "the beautiful" were one and the same. Brooks writes of Housman's poem: "Nature, for all her attractiveness to man, is supremely indifferent to him. This is the bedrock fact upon which the poem comes to rest, but if the fact constitutes a primal irony, it is accepted in this poem without rancor or any fierce bitterness."[22] The acceptance is beautiful as a certain behavior, but Brooks doesn't say so. Lane writes as if irony and the beautiful were the same, but he does not give reasons that cover the case.

Nor has he seen that Housman's irony—to call it that rather than beauty—stops short of his own presence in the landscape. Empson thinks the poem beautiful, but he recognizes as a problem the fact that Housman exempts himself from his own irony. Empson can't explain how such a childish attitude can still leave a poem intact:

> I think the poem is wonderfully beautiful. But a
> secret gimmick may well be needed in it to overcome
> our resistances, because the thought must be about

the silliest or most self-centred that has ever been expressed about Nature. Housman is offended with the scenery, when he pays a visit to his native place, because it does not remember the great man; this is very rude of it. But he has described it as a lover, so in a way the poem is only consistent to become jealous at the end.[23]

The jealous stanza is the last one:

> For nature, heartless, witless nature,
>   Will neither care nor know
> What stranger's feet may find the meadow
>   And trespass there and go,
> Nor ask amid the dews of morning
>   If they are mine or no.[24]

Jealousy may be a sufficient gimmick, and if it is, we can hardly complain about the degree of it in "heartless, witless," "stranger's feet," and "trespass." But it should make a problem for Lane, who seems to think that the beauty of the poem is the sole consideration and that it subsumes everything negative that one might, like Empson, say about it. It makes a problem for anyone who insists, beyond a reasonable degree, on the autonomy of the object claimed for beauty. Beauty may seem to cover every detail, as Lane evidently thinks, but the claim should not be pushed to the point of insisting that every detail is impeccable. Empson, too, wants to save the poem for beauty, and he has found in forgivable jealousy an excuse for saving it. He extends the human situation, on Housman's behalf, to include the natural silliness of being jealous, and so manages to save all the appearances. Jealousy is ugly, but it is too natural in a lover to be unacceptable.

But I still wonder about rescuing the beautiful from the menace of the pretty. The distinction is puritanically glib. There are forms of beauty which don't turn away from the pretty as resolutely as Lane supposes. T. J. Clark, writing of Pissarro, speaks of his hairshirt years and of his coming to terms at last with motives the hairshirt had not expunged: "Painting is hedonism, after all. It is profoundly nostalgic. It should not pretend that what it offers as beauty is entirely different from what its receivers call prettiness."[25] That seems a wiser comment, especially coming from subtle recognitions of Monet, Cézanne, Pissarro, and Renoir.

II

Interest in beauty and aesthetics was greatly stimulated in the first years of the twentieth century—as C. K. Ogden, I. A. Richards, and James Wood noted in *The Foundations of Aesthetics* (1922)—by a wider knowledge of non-European art, especially of Eastern and primitive art, and by the rapid development of psychology as an accredited practice. You could not assume any longer that the people who made cave drawings, tribal fetishes, or the "Stele of King Zet" did not know what they were doing and must have stumbled upon a skill since they could not have been artists. Richards (as I'll call the co-authors for short) spoke up for the new recognitions. He emphasized that there are many possible theories of beauty and outlined sixteen of them to represent decent opinion. The merit of listing them is that you're less likely to be oppressed by any one of them. Anything is beautiful which (1) possesses the simple quality of Beauty, (2) has a specified Form, (3) is an imitation of Nature, (4) results from successful exploitation of a medium, (5) is a work of Genius, (6) reveals (a) Truth, (b) the Spirit of Nature, (c) the Ideal, (d) the Universal, (e) the Typical, (7) produces illusion, (8) leads to desirable social effects, (9) is an expression, (10) causes pleasure, (11) excites emotions, (12) promotes a specific emotion, (13) involves the processes of empathy, (14) heightens vitality, (15) brings us into touch with exceptional personalities, or (16) conduces to synaesthesis. This last one is the only theory that Richards fully approved of, though he found some value in other ones, notably in (15) because "art is a means of establishing relations with personalities not otherwise accessible." The theory of synaesthesis is fulfilled when the impulses aroused by contemplating a work of art are so adjusted as to "preserve free play to every impulse, with entire avoidance of frustration." The difference between equilibrium (or balance) and irresolution is that in equilibrium "the impulses active, however they are specifically related, do yet sustain one state of mind." They combine "to produce one phase of consciousness." In irresolution "the sets of impulses sustain severally their independent phases." The organism veers between one phase of consciousness and another. Balance, the better state, is "a conflict of impulses solving itself in the arousal of the other impulses of the personality: [it] tends to bring the whole of the personality into play." Deadlock is the opposite of balance; the impulses trip one another up, causing only frustration. In any equilibrium of this kind, however momentary, Richards says, "we are experiencing beauty."[26] In other books he compares the vitality of synaesthesis to the central nervous system of a body in good working order, receiving diverse impulses and keeping the organism dancing.

It may be useful to retain Richards's sixteen theories while putting them into a different set of categories and adding a few of my own instances:

(A) Beauty as a property of the object in question

This would include Richards's theories 1, 2, 3, 4, and 6, fairly represented by two remarks of Coleridge's, which Richards quotes. The first is from "On Poesy or Art":

> The artist must imitate that which is within the thing, that which is active through form and figure, and discourses to us by symbols—the *Natur-Geist*, or spirit of nature, as we unconsciously imitate those we love; for so only can he hope to produce any work truly natural in the object and truly human in the effect.[27]

The second is from "On the Principles of Genial Criticism," where Coleridge in Kantian tones distinguishes the beautiful from the agreeable (which is beneath it) and the good (which is above it):

> The Mystics meant the same, when they define beauty as the subjection of matter to spirit so as to be transformed into a symbol, in and through which the spirit reveals itself; and declare *that* the *most* beautiful, where the most obstacles to a full manifestation have been most perfectly overcome.[28]

A few more exemplifications. Hazlitt, separating himself from Reynolds's notion that beauty was entirely dependent on custom or on "the conformity of objects to a given standard," noted that "there is also a certain conformity of objects to themselves, a symmetry of parts, a principle of proportion, gradation, harmony (call it what you will), which makes certain things naturally pleasing or beautiful, and the want of it the contrary."[29] In Joyce's *A Portrait of the Artist as a Young Man* Stephen Dedalus tries to explain to his friend Lynch that "Art . . . is the human disposition of sensible or intelligible matter for an aesthetic end," and he resorts to Aquinas's aphorism that "Pulchra sunt quae visa placent," translating the three qualities required for beauty—Aquinas's *integritas, consonantia,* and *claritas*—as "wholeness, harmony and radiance."[30] These are properties of the object, but someone must be in their presence to apprehend them. Here is the place for Balthasar's aesthetic theology, with its emphasis on "the transcendental origin of the beautiful" and "all the concrete kinds of beauty immanent in the world." It is no contradiction in Balthasar that he emphasizes the correspondence of the "external harmony" and "subjective need," the relation by which subjectivity, with its feeling and imagination, "frees itself in an objective work, in which it rediscovers itself," and in the course of which "there may be as much self-discovery as experience of another."[31] But the external world, God's creation, takes precedence. Hopkins and Ruskin take this precedence on faith. I would place in the present category, too, Edward S. Casey's distinction between the work of art and the aesthetic object: "The work of art is the perduring structural foundation for the aesthetic object. It has a constant being which is not dependent on being perceived, while the aesthetic object exists only as appearance, that is, only as experienced by the spectator. . . . As aesthetically perceived, the work of art *becomes* an aesthetic object.[32] Henri Focillon's *The Life of Forms in Art* holds that the life is visible in the forms: the forms are what we should be attending to. Leonard Meyer's emphasis on "relational richness" in a work of art would also come in here, his analysis of the Trio from the Minuetto movement of Mozart's G-minor Symphony (K. 550) being the most persuasive evidence of this property I have found.[33] Clive Bell's theory of Significant Form would fit, too, if he dropped "Significant" from it—"significant of what?"—and stuck to formalism. Baudelaire's "La Beauté" takes a similar position: the poem has the goddess find her force in stone, even if it is stone in which poets find mirrors to make all things more beautiful, "Mes yeux, mes larges yeux aux clartés éternelles!" Meanwhile, she exerts a classic, hieratic conviction on the poise of line and discretion:

Je hais le mouvement qui déplace les lignes,
Et jamais je ne pleure et jamais je ne ris.[34]

(B) Beauty as a quality—"genius"—of the artist

This would include Richards's theories 5, 9, and 15. He takes Croce's *Estetica* as the most influential version of this "expressionism," and he criticizes it for allowing any and every intuition to be expressive; therefore, "too many things become Art."[35] Croce wasn't troubled by that consideration; he believed that the distinction between a work of art and other things is "empirical and impossible to define." Richards thought that Croce, "preoccupied with the metaphysics of creative idealism," brought a serious theory to the absurd conclusion that an aphorism, a word, a syllable could be Art: he merely exploited "the suggestive powers of accepted phrases."[36] I would add, to document this set of theories, the "Hymne à la beauté" in which Baudelaire, for the moment a disciple of Poe, celebrates beauty not as the calm of classic statues but as impartial access to good and evil. Infinity and Totality seem to be one and the same. The personified Beauty might just as well be called Imagination or Genius, taking equal pleasure in conceiving Heaven and Hell. I quote the last four stanzas:

Tu marches sur des morts, Beauté, dont tu te moques;
De tes bijoux l'Horreur n'est pas le moins charmant,
Et le Meurtre, parmi tes plus chères breloques,
Sur ton ventre orgueilleux danse amoureusement.

L'éphémère ébloui vole vers toi, chandelle,
Crépite, flambe et dit: Bénissons ce flambeau!
L'amoureux pantelant incliné sur la belle
A l'air d'un moribond caressant son tombeau.

Que tu viennes du ciel ou de l'enfer, qu'importe,
O Beauté! monstre énorme, effrayant, ingénu!
Si ton oeil, ton souris, ton pied, m'ouvrent la porte
D'un Infini que j'aime et n'ai jamais connu?

De Satan ou de Dieu, qu'importe? Ange ou Sirène,
Qu'importe, si tu rends—fée aux yeux de velours,
Rythme, parfum, lueur, ô mon unique reine!—
L'univers moins hideux et les instants moins lourds?[37]

(C) Beauty as an experience of the perceiver

Psychology brings this forward, as in Richards's theories 7, 10,
11, 12, 13, 14, and 16. The gist of the wrong ones—all of them
except 16, Richards says,—is Bell's idea that works of art are
"the objects that provoke a particular emotion (aesthetic emotion)."[38] Samuel Alexander posits in each of us an "aesthetic impulse." Beauty or the beautiful is what satisfies the impulse to
beauty. The constructive impulse is diverted from practice "and
becomes contemplative."[39] Inevitably, Bell's version sends theorists off trying to find some quality common or peculiar to all
the objects that provoke the aesthetic emotion. There is no such
quality, Richards claims: the search for it is a superstition about
causes and effects. All I know is that what moves me, moves me.
This consideration does not invalidate Schiller's project on the
aesthetic education of mankind. It is reasonable to try to go from
adjective to noun, particle to principle. But it is superstitious
to try to find the principle—Beauty—embodied in one quality.

Richards is gruff about this set of theories, mainly, I think, because they muddy the psychological waters he has a particular interest in keeping clean. He is a psychologist who finds his choice problems and evidences in language, literature, logic, and aesthetics. He is interested in beauty because other people, too, are interested in it. Who they are, he doesn't quite say. He shares Tolstoy's belief that art should have universal reach or at least wide availability, and he quotes to good effect "Lo, Victress on the Peaks," a gorgeous poem in which Whitman addresses the spirit of Victory at the end of the Civil War:

> Lo, in these hours supreme,
> No poem proud, I chanting bring to thee, nor mastery's
>   rapturous verse,
> But a cluster containing night's darkness and
>   blood-dripping wounds,
> And psalms of the dead.[40]

But Richards doesn't say how, in a mass civilization, everyone can be expected to appreciate the beautiful and to have his psychic organizations stimulated by art to maintain dynamic balance. It is probably too much to look for. Meyer takes a more feasible position, as a theorist of music who puts his trust in competence. A competent listener, he says, is "one who understands the style of a work, not in the sense of knowing about—of conceptualizing—grammatical means, syntactic structures, or formal procedures, but in the sense that he has internalized the probabilities of the style as a set of perceptual, cognitive habits of discrimination and response."[41]

(D) Beauty valued for some further or extraneous reason

Richards's theory 8 has in view the insistence of Tolstoy, Ruskin, Morris, and John Middleton Murry that art should be beneficent work that blesses him who gives and him who receives. The theory seems to accept, with regret, the liberation of the beautiful from the true and the good, and to wonder how any free engagement with the beautiful can avoid being trivial. Richards names Hogarth's "The March to Finchley" as a case in point. I would add any works of religious or social edification such as the *Calvary* of Veronese, Georges de la Tour's *Saint Joseph the Carpenter*, and Delacroix's *Liberty Leading the People*.

III

A few trial sentences. Beauty is a value, to be perceived in its diverse manifestations. Aesthetics is the theory of such perception. Aesthetics and the theory of beauty are not the same, because the theory of beauty may be concentrated on objects and appearances, but aesthetics is concerned with perceptions and perceivers. Usually, aesthetics is labor shared among philosophers and psychologists. So far as it is thought about more commonly and unprofessionally, it seems to be regarded as a vacation exercise, a luxury, leisure activity for the middle and upper classes. But it is possible to take a quite different view of it, at least in the field of education and therefore of politics. Schiller gives us warrant for this. In his twentieth letter he says that every phenomenon may be thought of in four different connections:

> A thing may relate directly to our sensuous condition (our being and well-being); that is its *physical* character. Or it can relate to our reason, and furnish

us with knowledge; that is its *logical* character. Or it can relate to our will, and be regarded as an object of choice for a rational being; that is its *moral* character. Or finally, it can relate to the totality of our various powers, without being a specific object for any single one of them; that is its *aesthetic* character. . . . This last has as its aim the cultivation of the whole of our sensuous and intellectual powers in the fullest possible harmony.[42]

Those people are entirely right, Schiller acknowledges, "who declare the Beautiful, and the mood into which it transports our spirit, to be wholly indifferent and sterile in relation to *knowledge* and *mental outlook*." They are right, because beauty "gives no individual result whatever, either for the intellect or for the will; it realizes no individual purpose, either intellectual or moral; it discovers no individual truth, helps us to perform no individual duty, and is, in a word, equally incapable of establishing the character and clearing the mind." At this point, Schiller has made all the concessions he is willing to make: "A man's personal worth or dignity, then, insofar as this can depend upon himself, remains completely undetermined by aesthetic culture, and nothing more has been accomplished except that it has been rendered possible for him *on the part of Nature* to make of himself what he chooses—that he has had completely restored to him the freedom to be what he ought to be."[43]

This freedom is the highest gift, the gift of humanity. Beauty as a value is "our second creator," comparable to our first, who "similarly conferred on us nothing beyond the capacity for humanity, but left its exercise to our own volition." Every other exercise gives the mind "some particular aptitude" but also imposes a particular limitation. Only the aesthetic makes us free of our passions and predilections. We come to our freedom through beauty; beauty is "freedom in its appearance" (*erscheinende Frei-heit*).

Such freedom, in Schiller's version of it, is comparable to the artist's freedom in subduing the material with which he is dealing:

> In a truly beautiful work of art the content should do nothing, the form everything; for the wholeness of Man is affected by the form alone, and only individual powers by the content. However sublime and comprehensive it may be, the content always has a restrictive action upon the spirit, and only from the form is true aesthetic freedom to be expected. Therefore, the real artistic secret of the master consists in his *annihilating the material by means of the form*.[44]

I don't think this way of putting the question of content and form resolves an incorrigible issue. The dualism remains, and it is regrettable. In looking at a work of art, we are impelled to think of distinguishing content and form, only to decide not to do so. The single-minded work is in front of us. Perhaps form is achieved content rather than subdued content, a notion that unfortunately goes against every Schillerian motive. He would not allow us to see the content of the work redeemed or condoned, its "restrictive action upon the spirit" being as authoritarian as it is.

Schiller's ideal image of beauty, as in a beautiful society, is a "well executed English dance, composed of many complicated figures and turns." In a letter of February 23, 1793, to Christian Körner, he writes:

> A spectator located on the balcony observes an infinite variety of criss-crossing motions which keep

decisively but arbitrarily changing directions without ever colliding with each other. Everything has been arranged in such a manner that each dancer has already vacated his position by the time the other arrives. Everything fits so skillfully, yet so spontaneously, that everyone seems to be following his own lead, without ever getting in anyone's way. Such a dance is the perfect symbol of one's own individually asserted freedom as well as of one's respect for the freedom of the other.[45]

I will mention, briefly, because I have adverted to it in *The Practice of Reading,* another theory that takes the aesthetic as a comprehensive rather than an ancillary term: Louise M. Rosenblatt's theory of reading. She distinguishes between "efferent reading," in which "the reader's attention is focused on what he will take away from the transaction," and "aesthetic reading," in which the reader's attention is focused on what he or she "is living through during the reading event."[46] It is a distinction between reading for the gist of the text, or the plot of the novel, and reading for the whole experience of the words, first to last. Efferent reading goes with speed reading, flicking the eyes down the page. Aesthetic reading is the slowest reading possible, making provisional organizations of the meanings as we read, construing words not only for their local meaning but for the experience of their mutual bearing and torsion. There is always the possibility (and the risk) that the experience will change our lives.

Here is a poem by Herrick, "Upon Julia's Voice":

> So smooth, so sweet, so silv'ry is thy voice,
> As, could they hear, the Damn'd would make no noise,
> But listen to thee, (walking in thy chamber)
> Melting melodious words, to Lutes of Amber.[47]

It may not change anyone's life, but reading it aesthetically will clear a little space in one's mind for disinterestedness. An efferent reading is not worth bringing away, as it amounts to little more than *you have a beautiful voice*. But the poem is not as simple as it looks. A modern editor glosses the last line: ". . . to the accompaniment of lutes inlaid either with amber, the fossilized resin, or with amber, the alloy made of four parts silver to one of gold. . . . What Herrick probably intends is that the silver of her voice melts with the golden words to produce musical sounds (like those from lutes), which are thus a musical alloy analogous to metallic amber."[48] The first of these possibilities seems enough to me. Herrick doesn't say that Julia's words are golden; they are melodious. Melting them means dissolving them into silence; silence transformed by her voice such that—as in Eliot's "The Dry Salvages"—the music is "heard so deeply / That it is not heard at all, but you are the music / While the music lasts."[49] The first line, So A, So B, So C, is standard analogical hyperbole to get the tribute going, but it takes the opportunity of rhyming "voice" with "noise" and sets Herrick thinking of the howling Damn'd. The hyperbole runs so far as to suggest that even the damned in Hell could be redeemed if they were to listen to Julia's voice and share the silence into which her words reach. There is also a suggestion, according to a different tradition of myth, that Julia's voice is Orpheus's in a minor key. The first line has the merit of starting a common pattern of phrase that does not need to be repeated: it is good enough to depart from, as in the second line. The poem is beautiful for various reasons: the sinuousness of its rhythm; the propriety with which the speaker, having with the first line apparently come to the end of his adjectival resources, withdraws into the winding cadence of "As, could they hear, the Damn'd would make no noise, / But listen to thee"; the grace with which he stays within his limitations and those of his style, giving it only the small virtues. The grammar with its sequence of subjunctives—"could they hear," "would make no noise," "but listen"—sends the sentence across the first couplet into the second one, establishing a countermelody without chastening the rhyme. The rhyme of "voice" and "noise" sounds the dramatic contrast of the couplet, but the sentence goes on its longer way, hovering in the middle of the third line, where the two present participles (one of them in parentheses) direct it to the setting of the accompanying lutes. The first couplet is entirely monosyllabic. The second, with its mixture of monosyllables and disyllables—"listen," "walking," "chamber"—sustains the alliterative flourish of "Making melodious words" before it subsides to the novel rhyme of "chamber" and "Amber." The poem is at one with the music it alludes to. Herrick has learned as much from Dowland as from Ovid.

Is what I have said enough to indicate that Herrick's poem is beautiful, and why it is? No, though I have no right to say "of course not," since someone else might do better with it and fail not as completely. I can only place beside the poem companionable words just as abstract as "beauty": sinuousness, propriety, grace. I cannot define beauty or the beautiful. I can point to certain details and hope you will take my word for them as manifestations of beauty categorically undefined if not indefinable. I settle for saying the little I can say, and consign the remainder to an implicative silence, taking some cold comfort from a few remarks of E. M. Cioran: "The identity of a word conceals a number of divergent experiences." The divergences can't be allowed for in any sentence. "The indigence of language renders the universe intelligible." [50] Or, rather: gives us the illusion that the universe is intelligible.

IV

So far, I've been speaking of beauty as a value, a good, even allowing for disagreements on particular objects that seem beautiful to someone but not to someone else. But it is possible to disapprove of beauty in principle, and to think it a nuisance; because it impedes other practices you find more important; because talk of beauty is a distraction, confounding other vocabularies; or because you take beauty seriously only in a particular context of discourse. I'll mention three dissidents.

Paul de Man regularly spoke of beauty and the aesthetic as his enemies, all the more sinister for their pretending to be innocuous. In "Aesthetic Formalization in Kleist" he argued that "it is as a political force that the aesthetic still concerns us as one of the most powerful ideological drives to act upon the reality of history." He resented Schiller's claim that the aesthetic is at once nothing and everything; that by virtue of its exerting no local influence it governs every observance: it is the dance along the artery. "What gives the aesthetic its power," de Man claimed, "and hence its practical, political impact, is its intimate link with knowledge, the epistemological implications that are always in play when the aesthetic appears over the horizon of discourse."[51] The aesthetic claims to know nothing, but it also claims the wisdom of being beyond knowledge, or on the far side of it, in full possession of the self-evidence of human feeling and therefore having unique access to the universal patterns of human life. So de Man brought Kleist's puppets to exert their deconstructive pressure on the piety of Schiller's English dance: the puppets are "cleansed from the pathos of self-consciousness as well as from the disruptions and ironies of imitation." For the dancing puppets, "there is no risk of affectation (*Ziererei*), of letting the aesthetic effect be determined by the dynamics of the represented passion or emotion rather than by the formal laws of tropes."[52]

It is a pity, de Man doesn't quite say, that a puppet-master is necessary and that his fingers express his will.

T. J. Clark, who can be explicit but often prefers to remain cryptic, has an astonishing sentence in *Farewell to an Idea:* "It is the reason we all hate the beautiful so much." He has been talking about the version of Cézanne's *Bathers* in Philadelphia and offering to explain why even the best critics of Cézanne— Roger Fry and Meyer Schapiro—recoil from it. They sense an "inorganic chill" in the air of the painting, its refusal to be entirely humane, vibrant, tense, or sensitive. Their effort is vain, Clark claims. He says of the painting: "No handling has ever been less a means of laying hold of (getting one's hands on) a human world." Why? So far as I understand him, he appears to say that one dream of materialism is to give examples of "our being in the world and having knowledge of it." This dream seeks the "patient disclosure of a world." But materialism has another dream, like that of Kleist's puppeteer, in which human volition is removed from the marionettes and the dance goes on as if inanimate matter were triumphant without recourse to us. Clark argues that while this is not a description of Cézanne's *Bathers*, it describes a "logic that threatens to overtake them." What is most touching in *Bathers* is "their will to resist the vision of bodies that the pictures' own ruthlessness makes possible." Their ruthlessness, I gather, is a property of Cézanne's divining, while going about his humane and mimetic business, an alien possibility—negative, cold, puppet-like—which his vision at once assented to and rejected. So Clark speaks of the "necessary other dream of materialism—the one to which the various (but limited) mechanisms we call aesthetic give access, and from which we regularly draw back." Aesthetics presumably allows us to dream this second dream but prevents us from yielding to it. "It is the reason we all hate the beautiful so much." One is inclined to say to Clark: speak for yourself. But he is speaking for himself and for those who resent the force of the beautiful which keeps them imprisoned in its glowing appearances; does not let them indulge themselves in the horrific dream of seeing matter taking over the world, expunging self-consciousness, pathos, and desire alike, the whole sensitive mess since life began.

Modernism, according to Clark, is doomed to have the double vision of beauty and its deadly other:

> Modernism, I am convinced, would not anger its opponents in the way it seems to if it did not so flagrantly assert the beautiful as its ultimate commitment. And if it did not repeatedly discover the beautiful as nothing but mechanism, nothing but matter dictating (dead) form. This is a horrible proposal, and I understand and sympathize with the desire to retrieve the human, the social, and the discursive on the other side of it. I too would like there to have been a sane (that is, surviving) van Gogh to cancel Seurat's nihilism, or a truly clever Marcel Duchamp to save us from Malevich's divine idiocy. But it turns out there was neither. This is modernism's worst discovery.[53]

But it may still be possible to mitigate the harm of this discovery. Clark's chapter on Jackson Pollock does not claim that modernism discovered the beautiful as nothing but mechanism, matter dictating (dead) form. In a commentary on Pollock's *Number 1, 1948*, Clark refers to the "central black whiplash with its gorgeous bleep of red, and the final black spot to the right of it."[54] Yes, it is gorgeous, and however we fail to elucidate its beauty, we cannot talk of mechanisms in command or of matter dictating (dead) form. I think the explanation of Clark's susceptibility to beauty and his determination to hate it is clarified by a remarkable passage he quotes from Longinus: "Homer forces and compels into unnatural union prepositions which are not easily joined together when he says 'from under death.' He has tortured his line into conformity with the impending disaster . . . and almost stamps upon the words the very shape of the peril: 'they are carried from under death.'"[55] Clark likes to torture his sense of beauty into conformity with the impending triumph of mechanism, even though it is a triumph he is not finally willing to celebrate. He loves to come upon an art that drives itself to the end of its tether and tempts itself with the formal thrill of negation. Perhaps he thinks of beauty as settling too easily upon unions of preposition and noun, and of aesthetics as theorizing such unions in favor of an ideology of nature.

Balthasar's dissidence is more radical than de Man's or Clark's, if only because he aims to develop a theological aesthetics, a "Christian theology in the light of the third transcendental—that is to say: to complement the vision of the true and the good with that of the beautiful (*pulchrum*)." He wants to make the *pulchrum* appear "in its rightful place within the total ordered structure, namely as the manner in which God's goodness (*bonum*) gives itself and is expressed by God and understood by man as the truth (*verum*)." Balthasar deplores the fact that theology has dispensed with the beautiful and that the true, the good, and the beautiful have been separated so that each may go its different way:

> Beauty is the word that shall be our first. Beauty is the last thing which the thinking intellect dares to approach, since only beauty dances as uncontained splendour around the double constellation of the true and the good and their inseparable relation to one another. Beauty is the disinterested one, without which the ancient world refused to understand itself, a word which imperceptibly and yet unmis-

takably has bade farewell to our new world, a world of interests, leaving it to its own avarice and sadness. No longer loved or fostered by religion, beauty is lifted from its face as a mask, and its absence exposes features on that face which threaten to become incomprehensible to man. We no longer dare to believe in beauty and we make of it a mere appearance in order the more easily to dispose of it.[56]

The elimination of aesthetics from theology and from the whole Christian life has entailed "the expulsion of contemplation from the act of faith, the exclusion of 'seeing' from 'hearing,' the removal of the *inchoatio visionis* from the *fides*, and the relegation of the Christian to the old age which is passing away."[57]

Balthasar is not interested in promoting aesthetics as a separate consideration or a nuanced enthusiasm. He finds it appalling that as a consequence of the autonomy of the sciences and philosophy, the beautiful has been "lifted from the unreflected position within a totality which it had enjoyed from the days of the Greeks and made into a separate 'object' with a separate science of its own." This consequence "can be detected as early as the Renaissance, but later on it emerges in full force with Bruno and Shaftesbury." And most unfortunately in Herder and Kierkegaard. Kierkegaard's *Stages on Life's Way* distinguishes the "apostle" and the "martyr of truth" from the "genius" and thereby eradicates from theology all traces of an aesthetic attitude.[58] Separated from ethics and logic, "what we are used to calling 'aesthetic' is as tinged with the vanity and unreality of original sin as is (enlightened) reason."[59] Inevitably, Catholic and Protestant followers of Kierkegaard use the word "aesthetic" to denote an attitude "which, in the last analysis, they find to be frivolous, merely curious and self-indulgent."[60]

In Balthasar's theological aesthetics, the beautiful, the true, and the good are found in full and simultaneous companionship. We may speak of one of these, if only because we have to refer to one thing at a time, but we should not think of one in isolation from the other two. Subject to this presence of mind, we can emphasize one value or another:

> The aesthetic experience is the union of the greatest possible concreteness of the individual form and the greatest possible universality of its meaning or of the epiphany within it of the mystery of Being. The most powerful experience of it outside of Christianity, furthermore, connects this epiphany with place and time, with a *kairos,* a happening: in the appearance of a god the divine has approached men and become manifest to them.[61]

In Christianity:

> The quality of "being-in-itself" which belongs to the beautiful, the demand the beautiful itself makes to be allowed to be what it is, the demand, therefore, that we renounce our attempts to control and manipulate it, in order truly to be able to be happy by enjoying it: all of this is, in the natural realm, the foundation and foreshadowing of what in the realm of revelation and grace will be the attitude of faith.[62]

It follows that Balthasar interprets the lexicon of aesthetics and the beautiful under the sign of faith, and gives each word the transformed value it would have if the true, the good, and the beautiful amounted to one comprehensive act of faith. The familiar mood of enthusiasm, for instance, would not merely be adjectival to the person who feels it while looking, say, at a work of art:

Before the beautiful—no, not really *before* but *within* the beautiful—the whole person quivers. He not only "finds" the beautiful moving; rather, he experiences himself as being moved and possessed by it. The more complete this experience is, the less does a person seek and enjoy only the delight that comes through the senses or even through any act of his own; the less also does he reflect on his own acts and states. Such a person has been taken up wholesale into the reality of the beautiful and is now fully subordinate to it, determined by it, animated by it.[63]

In similar spirit, Balthasar reinterprets the "subjective judgment of taste" not as a faculty content with its spontaneity but by appeal to a sacramental understanding of the object to which it is directed:

By developing his soul according to the images of the objectively beautiful, the maturing person gradually learns to acquire the art of discrimination, that is, the art of perceiving what is beautiful in itself. In the process of their development, the subjective elements of perception (which, doubtless, include state of mind and fantasy) more and more pass into the service of objective perception.[64]

What must be guarded against is "aestheticism," a practice Balthasar can only view with dismay.

V

This recital of attitudes and values may be exhausting, but it is not exhaustive. I've given only samples. My aim is not to reach a clarification, worse still a premature one, but to suggest how words and sentences about beauty may be construed in different contexts, many of them hard to live up to. Balthasar's is probably the most arduous of these. If we took him as seriously as he deserves, we would have to change our lives. But even if we didn't go that far, reading his books would have the salutary effect of making the visible a little hard to see; we would be less sanguine in engaging with its deliverances. For instance: my comments on the passage I quoted from *Mrs. Dalloway* implied that my only obligation as a reader is to enter into the spirit of Peter Walsh's pleasure, on that summer evening in London. I am supposed to assent, at least for the time being, to the universal ambition of beauty, its zeal in encompassing—or appearing to encompass— the whole of experience. I mentioned other disciplines than the aesthetic, such as politics, sociology, and psychology, but I did not think that any of these should be allowed to intimidate the aesthetic sense or the sense of beauty. I saw no reason to obstruct Peter's access to the flare and glare. But suppose I adverted to Balthasar's admonition: "we no longer dare to believe in beauty and we make of it a mere appearance in order the more easily to dispose of it." What else does Peter Walsh do—or Virginia Woolf, for that matter—than make of beauty a mere appearance? Not necessarily to dispose of it—there is no evidence of that intention. But he is entirely willing to have one parade of appearances replaced by another. He places himself at the point where he can best see the parade, and he enjoys it, but he does not ask that the appearances do anything more than minister to his satisfaction. He does not invoke the true and the good to make, with the beautiful, a triple value more profound than any one of its particles. It may seem eccentric to bring up Balthasar's big gun while reading a transitional paragraph of Virginia Woolf's prose, but there is no good reason to block off impingements or take precautions against seeing further aspects of her writing.

2

The Tragic Sense of Beauty

I

"The Tragic Generation" was Yeats's phrase to denote a loose fellowship of his friends, writers, and artists who sought Beauty not only as an end in itself but as the primary value to which they committed themselves. In his *Autobiographies*, he tried to explain why these men—his friends in London in the 1890s—fell into dissipation and chaos. He was thinking particularly of Lionel Johnson and Ernest Dowson, but Wilde, Beardsley, Arthur Symons, and Stenbock were not far from his mind. His first thoughts on the question prompted him to quote some lines from his poem "Ego Dominus Tuus." In the poem, one of the disputants maintains that

> . . . those that love the world serve it in action,
> Grow rich, popular and full of influence,
> And should they paint or write, still it is action:
> The struggle of the fly in marmalade.
> The rhetorician would deceive his neighbours,
> The sentimentalist himself; while art
> Is but a vision of reality.
> What portion in the world can the artist have
> Who has awakened from the common dream
> But dissipation and despair?

I take that last question as a more pointed version of Wordsworth's lines in "Resolution and Independence":

We Poets in our youth begin in gladness;
But thereof comes in the end despondency and
madness.[1]

In "The Tragic Generation," after quoting the lines from "Ego
Dominus Tuus," Yeats offers a theory of English poetry that
starts with Spenser's islands of Phaedria and Acrasia. "In those
islands," he says, "certain qualities of beauty, certain forms of
sensuous loveliness were separated from all the general purposes
of life, as they had not been hitherto in European literature—
and would not be again, for even the historical process has its
ebb and flow, till Keats wrote his *Endymion.*" "I think," he continues, "that the movement of our thought has more and more
so separated certain images and regions of the mind, and that
these images grow in beauty as they grow in sterility." Yeats then
develops this idea into a social theory of English literature and
drama:

> Shakespeare leaned, as it were, even as craftsman,
> upon the general fate of men and nations, had about
> him the excitement of the playhouse; and all poets,
> including Spenser in all but a few pages, until our
> age came, and when it came almost all, have had
> some propaganda or traditional doctrine to give
> companionship with their fellows. Had not Mat-
> thew Arnold his faith in what he described as the
> best thought of his generation, Browning his psy-
> chological curiosity, Tennyson, as before him Shel-
> ley and Wordsworth, moral values that were not aes-
> thetic values?

At that point in his theory, Yeats thinks of another fellowship
of poets, antithetical to those he has named: "But Coleridge of
the 'Ancient Mariner' and 'Kubla Khan,' and Rossetti in all his

writings, made what Arnold has called that 'morbid effort,' that search for 'perfection of thought and feeling, and to unite this to perfection of form,' sought this new, pure beauty, and suffered in their lives because of it."[2]

In "The Autumn of the Body" Yeats speaks of the search for this new, pure beauty as an "ever more arduous search for an almost disembodied ecstasy."[3] When we turn back to the lines from "Ego Dominus Tuus," we know that by "the world" Yeats means reality as we have been instructed to yield to it, and that by the "common dream" he means what Shelley called the trance of real life, the delusion by which we think that reality coincides at every point with its appearances. We know, too, that Yeats's affection on this occasion goes out not to Arnold, Browning, and Tennyson but to the defeated poets, "those who more and more must make all out of the privacy of their thought, calling up perpetual images of desire," poets who suffer "from the terrors that pass before shut eyes."[4]

I have referred to that passage in Yeats's *Autobiographies* to suggest what it would mean if one were to take beauty seriously as a value, instead of thinking of it as charm or prettiness, felicities of the visible world. Not that the distinction between beauty and prettiness is absolute. But Yeats and his friends had to think it was, and that their fate was tragic in serving such a goddess. Symons's "Modern Beauty" recites the myth and the grim conditions it had to face:

> I am the torch, she saith, and what to me
> If the moth die of me? I am the flame
> Of Beauty, and I burn that all may see
> Beauty, and I have neither joy nor shame,
> But live with that clear life of perfect fire
> Which is to men the death of their desire.

I am Yseult and Helen, I have seen
Troy burn, and the most loving knight lie dead.
The world has been my mirror, time has been
My breath upon the glass; and men have said,
Age after age, in rapture and despair,
Love's poor few words, before my image there.

I live, and am immortal; in my eyes
The sorrow of the world, and on my lips
The joy of life, mingle to make me wise;
Yet now the day is darkened with eclipse:
Who is there lives for beauty? Still am I
The torch, but where's the moth that still dares die? [5]

In this poem, from Symons's *Images of Good and Evil* (1899), Beauty is a force of nature more than a force of culture. As in Pater's *Studies in the History of the Renaissance,* she is a flame of being: torch, fire, image. Divine, it is her tragedy that she must consent to live in the ordinary world and seek her devotees among people who have, as a general habit, more terrestrial interests. Who is there lives for beauty? Not many, but that hardly matters. It matters only that the goddess survive in memory, story, and the endlessness of desire.

This dedication was not confined to Yeats's friends. One of Emily Dickinson's poems gives Beauty only the companionship of a value in similar distress:

I died for Beauty—but was scarce
Adjusted in the Tomb
When One who died for Truth, was lain
In an adjoining Room—

He questioned softly "Why I failed"?
"For Beauty," I replied—

"And I—for Truth—Themself are One—
We Brethren, are," He said—

And so, as Kinsmen, met a Night—
We talked between the Rooms—
Until the Moss had reached our lips—
And covered up—our names— [6]

Themself, not themselves: they are, as in Keats's ode, one and the same, or kinsmen, sharing a common fate: "And covered up—our names." In Symons's poem at least the name persists and is worshipped by a few.

Yeats asks us not only to take Beauty seriously but to live under her sign. We may decide not to. We may think that the price of living in that way is exorbitant and the commitment to it vain. Like Balthasar, we may regard as disastrous the separation of truth, virtue, and beauty. The merit of this separation was that it dismissed false associations and glib analogies: "But the aesthetic had a strange power of attraction. When put aside, it does not rest until as myth, eros, framework of thought or Hegelian kingdom of ideas it comes finally to dominate all the rest, and to incorporate Christianity as a way to itself." [7]

But we should at least recognize that some people have been ready to devote themselves to beauty as to a supreme value, even if it entailed their being defeated by vulgar and sometimes by lofty forces. I have in mind the issues that Gissing engaged in *New Grub Street* and Henry James in "The Next Time," the difficulty of maintaining beauty and the highest demands of the imagination, given the sullen forces at large among the conditions of authorship. I am also thinking of the letter that James's Hyacinth Robinson sent the Princess Casamassima from Venice telling her that he had now come to appreciate "the splendid accumulations of the happier few, to which doubtless the miserable many have also in their degree contributed." These "monu-

ments and treasures of art, the great palaces and properties"
seemed to him "inestimably precious and beautiful," despite "all
the despotisms, the cruelties, the exclusions, the monopolies
and the rapacities of the past," and he wondered in dismay what
the princess and Poupin and other revolutionists proposed to do
with them.[8] This is to say that an aesthetic attitude may dissent
not only from the official definition of reality but from revolutionary plans to destroy it.

The main difficulty that oppressed writers in the later years
of the nineteenth century was not the stolidity of the broad-
backed public but the loss of a common discourse which serious writers could practice without humiliation. Arnold's cultural treasury, Browning's psychological curiosity, Tennyson's
moral values that were not aesthetic values: these served their
local purposes, but they did not make up for the loss of a common idiom that might support a wide range of feelings. John
Barrell has reported, in *The Political Theory of Painting from Reynolds to Hazlitt*, that after the generation of Hazlitt and Haydon, "no writer appears who still believes that the civic humanist discourse can be adapted so as to define a republic of taste
whose structure can replicate the structure of what is now recognized as a 'mass society.'" This is not to say that there were
no more attempts "to argue that a primary function of painting is to make us aware of what we have in common." But it is
significant, as Barrell remarks, that Ruskin, for example, "stakes
his claim for the unifying power of painting on the representation, not of the human body, but of landscape." Ruskin re-
gretted this development and regarded the nineteenth-century
preoccupation with landscape as a consequence of "mistakes in
our social economy," the expression of a love of liberty that could
no longer find satisfaction in civic life. Barrell remarks: "For
Ruskin, as for Reynolds, or Barry, or Fuseli, the history of painting is a political history; but for Ruskin, also, modern painting

is inevitably the place of privacy, of private freedom; however it may lead us back to the body of the public, it must first lead us away from it, to where we can 'lose the company of our friends among the hills.'"[9] A writer who was willing to lose such company took to the hills for the same reason that Yeats's friends in London huddled together to read their poems to one another in the Cheshire Cheese: they shared only the burden of being each private to himself. The poets who sought the new, pure beauty that Yeats referred to turned away from a degraded vernacular just as desperately as from the commonly declared purposes of human life. Some found the strategic retreat to landscape not at all reliable. Lyotard has argued that at the end of the nineteenth century, despite the efforts of speculative thought and Romanticism, "confidence in natural forms was shaken, and beyond forms or in their very depth, thought was made liable, *empfänglich*, for something that did not speak to it in good and due form."[10] Dissent seemed the only political response available to writers who were so alienated as to seek the new, pure beauty that Yeats described. It was silent dissent, but exemplary, and it remained dissent even if some of those writers voted Conservative and respected the Empire.

II

Taking beauty seriously has long been a difficult enterprise, mainly because it has been an equivocal value. In Plato, as in Greek thought generally, it was not found necessary to distinguish with any insistence the beautiful, the true, and the good. Plato took human beauty as the paradigm of this value; a far-reaching decision, because it made it more difficult to protect the beautiful person from being merely desired. In the *Symposium* you are admonished to begin with that desire and to purify it by yearning not for the boy's body but for the idea of Beauty it imperfectly adumbrates. But it was difficult to go beyond the flesh. Probably for that reason, modern theorists of Beauty took natural landscapes or works of art rather than boys as their paradigm. According to Plato, the beautiful, the true, and the good were available, as an Idea or an ideal Form, to the soul rather than to the senses: embodiments of those values were alike regarded as secondary to the eternal Form of each. If you started with one of them, you supposedly approached the other two, and without any feeling of discrepancy. Plato and Aristotle had in mind human perfection—they were not much concerned with flowers or vistas—and they used the rhetorical force of beauty, truth, and virtue for what they were worth. But if three values are said to be indistinguishable, sooner or later it will occur to someone to distinguish them. There will be some occasions on which it is rhetorically useful to emphasize one of them more than the other two. The values will be distinguished, but the distinctions will not hold for every context. The nouns may be separated, but the adjectives that qualify them will blur the entities separated. Plotinus is often credited with—or blamed for—the separation of beauty from its companions. The first and the fifth Books of his *Ennead* can be quoted in evidence, but he also held that "the Good, which lies beyond, is the Fountain at once and Principle of Beauty: the Primal Good and the Primal Beauty have the one dwelling-place and, thus, always Beauty's seat is There." [11] If you wanted to make beauty the first among three equal values, and to emphasize harmony and perfection of form in the beautiful object, you could invoke a tradition that includes Plotinus, Augustine, Boethius, and Aquinas, with Augustine's *De Musica* as an inspiring moment, but you would have to allow for a certain slippage among the three values.

Besides, the tradition is not of one mind or disposition. In the *Sophist* and the tenth Book of the *Republic* Plato depreciates art because it merely replicates what is already in the world, fully present and complete, however secondary the object is by comparison with the Idea. But you could propose a case for art by making it independent of objects to be imitated. You could recognize, as Cicero does in the *Laws* and Plotinus in the fifth Book of the *Ennead*, that Phidias sculpted his *Zeus* not by imitating anyone in the world but by consulting his own mind, finding there "a sublime notion of beauty," and sculpting that.[12] Phidias produced his *Zeus*, as Plotinus says, "according to nothing visible, but he made him such as Zeus himself would appear should he wish to reveal himself to our eyes."[13] This made it possible to think of the beauty of a work of art as independent of nature, and perhaps superior to nature to the extent to which a Platonic Idea floats free of its necessarily imperfect and partial manifestation. In the first Book of the *Ennead* Plotinus urges us to fly from sensory to intellectual beauty, because sensory beauty is merely the shadow of an image. Indeed, the neo-Platonic tradition pointed or could be directed toward a psychology of beauty, because only in one's mind could one intuit the Intellectual Beauty that was not the work of imitation. This makes a problem for Formalism, since no form can be better—in a Platonic sense—than penultimate. It also makes it hard to endow mere objects, the ordinary universe, with value. In a certain light every neo-Platonic emphasis seems tiresomely angelic, one of the "colder lunacies" that Empson writes of in "The Teasers," that "cheat the love, the moment, the small fact."[14] Some other tradition would have to be invoked if you wanted to treat a particular form of beauty as ultimate or to discourage any acts of Idealism in its presence. There are not many such traditions, if only because western philosophy from Plato to Heidegger has established itself on the primacy of being and knowledge. Ontology and epistemology have far more interest in "the true" than in "the beautiful" or "the good."

In medieval thought, the beautiful was in practice rarely distinguished from the true and the good: the posited integration of values made it unnecessary to separate one from the others.[15] Even when a theoretical distinction was proposed, what was asserted was the ultimate unity of being. No value was declared to be autonomous. By the eighteenth century, aesthetics was conducted, however tentatively, as a separate discipline. "The beautiful" was analyzed apart from "the true" and "the good." But there was no strict agreement on the character of aesthetics, except that most theorists regarded it as a special form of the theory of perception and therefore of mainly psychological interest. This partly explains why eighteenth-century theorists of beauty often seem to prefer to talk about something else to which beauty is loosely related. Addison, Hume, Hutcheson, Shaftesbury, and Burke evidently wanted to talk about common sense, taste, morality, certain prejudices or sentiments, community, psychology, natural law, or politics while apparently talking about beauty. Beauty provided them with a rhetorical occasion, but it was found impossible to name any quality common to every object they thought beautiful. You could say that a flower, a woman, a sonnet, a mathematical formula, or a piece of legislation was beautiful, but you could not make any more specific claim for its quality. Gradually through the century, Beauty was dislodged by a renewed interest in the Sublime and the subjective faculty of Taste. Burke's emphasis on the pain and pleasure of the Sublime made it impossible to exclude the ugly from aesthetic experience. The concept of "the expressive" included "the beautiful" but was far more comprehensive than that. Besides, the new interest in sensibility and psychology made it more fruitful—as in Addison, Gerard, and Burke—to talk about the forms of subjectivity than to keep on trying to list the objective properties of a beautiful thing. Hutcheson continued to recognize the objective properties, but he seemed old-fashioned in doing so. Shaftesbury, Addison, and Hutcheson in his revisionary mode adumbrated a theory of the aesthetic attitude rather than of the beautiful object, and they recommended the notion of disinterestedness as its main quality, the subjective correlative of what passed in the object for autonomy. It was as if they internalized dissent as the determination to stand aside from worldly purposes. They had a better chance of grounding an aesthetic in the subject, the viewer's attitude, than in any qualities of the objects looked at. They could present the viewer's mind dissociating itself for the time being from the standard social and political aims, possession and power. Within a few years the idea of disinterestedness became so common that Hogarth laughed at it in *The Analysis of Beauty* (1753).[16] But it was left to Kant to try to establish the aesthetic as an independent value.

Kant's immediate provocation was Baumgarten. In the *Meditationes Philosophicae* (1735) and the *Aesthetica* (1750) Baumgarten designated as aesthetic the action of sensory knowledge as distinct from logic. But he also proposed to bring "the beautiful" under the supervision of rational principles. Kant thought this a fruitless project and rejected it in a note to the first *Critique*. In the third *Critique* he put forward a crucial consideration, that "by an aesthetical idea I understand that representation of the imagination which occasions much thought, without however any definite thought, i.e. any *concept,* being capable of being adequate to it; it consequently cannot be completely compassed and made intelligible by language."[17] This sentence has foundational value in the history of aesthetics because it released judgments of taste from their being determinable by concepts: it relieved aesthetics from the oppression of ontology, epistemology, and morality. In Kant, the beautiful is serious because it symbolizes the good. But he kept them otherwise separate. If they were not kept separate, the beautiful (like the good) would be subject to moral and conceptual adjudication. For the same reason, Kant had to distinguish between free and adherent beauty, because adherent beauty is bound by the concept of what the particular thing—a man, a woman, a horse—should be. A horse should not look like a camel. Kant's theory of beauty is therefore concentrated on the natural world and on free beauty. Free beauty is subject only to a judgment of taste, a faculty which features the harmony of understanding and imagination: it is disinterested, irresponsible, as free as play. But a judgment of taste, according to Kant, is justified in asking to be universally accepted, because it can appeal to a *sensus communis,* which Kant claims as operative. The fact that in common practice the claim of taste is not accepted does not refute the claim. It follows from Kant's exposition of taste that the object of aesthetic attention is found in nature or in art and it comes into a judgment of taste by virtue of its form. It may include concepts—as in *King Lear,* "nothing will come of nothing"—but even if it does, the concepts are subsumed like every other constituent of the work in its form.

It was also a liberating moment on Kant's part when he said that "Beauty is the form of the *purposiveness* of an object, so far as this is perceived in it *without any representation of a purpose.*" But that liberty is qualified somewhat by Kant's finding instances of it in nature more clearly than in art. A tulip, he says, "is regarded as beautiful, because in perceiving it we find a certain purposiveness which, in our judgment, is referred to no purpose at all." [18] But I don't think it was a major theoretical problem to extend that recognition from tulips to works of art. You could explain the idea of purposiveness without purpose by saying that purposiveness is the attitude that never goes forward to any corresponding action: it is the finality encountered in the form of the beautiful object. The form is final; it does not lead beyond itself, it does not insist on a teleological or otherwise Platonic end. Kant's version of disinterestedness corresponds to the recognition of purposiveness without purpose. We are content to appreciate the beauty of the object and to retain that intuition.

I have mentioned autonomy, a quality that can be ascribed to people and to objects. If to people, it means that each of us is free to see things as we want to; though in that formulation the freedom may be questioned later on. Are we sure the freedom is genuine, or is it just an occult form of obedience to laws genetically or culturally inscribed? If autonomy is ascribed to an artist, it is a quality that embodies his genius, his authority to "set the example for others" less authoritative than he is.[19] If it is ascribed to objects, such as works of artistic beauty, it honors the degree to which the object—the work of art—has been invented in a zone of freedom: no formal constraint has been imposed. It is probable that the artist has discovered, in the process of the working, possibilities internal to the medium, far beyond the scope of any particular intention. It is unlikely that *Finnegans Wake* came out exactly as Joyce intended it when he wrote the first words.

Disinterestedness is usually ascribed to people rather than to objects. What does it mean? Some theorists regard it as an implausible value; they doubt that it can be maintained for long without yielding to one interest or another. It seems to me a feasible value, an attitude, a gesture of forbearance, a determination not to give in to the more clamorous interests that press upon it. By being disinterested, I clear a space for certain perceptions that would not survive in the marketplace. I cultivate a semblance of desire rather than yield to desire. But it is possible to interpret disinterestedness in several ways. You could take it as an attribute of the wealthy class, which can afford to treat life as a spectacle and to look at beautiful objects without committing the vulgarity of desiring them. As for desire, they could leave that to their servants. Disinterestedness could be presented as the conspicuous practice of a certain tone, like picnicking on the lawns at Glyndebourne. You could also see disinterestedness as featuring a certain tension between tragedy and hope. It is tragic if you construe it as a desperate device to evade the gross interests we are offered, desperate since you expect it to be defeated in the end: hopeful if you see it as holding out the possibility of a new politics, lodged as it is among other values with which it might be possible to cooperate. So you could take an expansive view of it. Adorno maintains that disinterestedness does not arise spontaneously but comes to us with a certain historical experience: "The disinterested pleasure that according to Kant is aroused by works of art can only be understood by virtue of historical antitheses still at work in each aesthetic object. The thing disinterestedly contemplated pleases because it once claimed the utmost interest and thus precluded contemplation. The latter is a triumph of enlightened self-discipline." Objects of disinterested contemplation, according to Adorno, offer promise of "a happiness cured of domination over nature." It follows that purposelessness "gives the lie to the totality of purposefulness in the world of domination." Only by virtue of this negation has modern society become aware of other negations that are possible: it is not always necessary to capitulate to the zeitgeist.[20] Schiller's concept of play as a factor in the aesthetic education of mankind follows expansively from Kant in these emphases.

Disinterestedness in the subject is a response to the implied autonomy of the object in view. The theory of autonomy holds to these axioms. A work of art is first and last an aesthetic semblance, a formal invention waiting to be perceived. It is to be valued as a redemptive example of the human character of work, performance, and production, as opposed to the instrumental reduction of work to labor characteristic of capitalist practices. It is also valued as an acknowledgment of the gratuitous character of certain experiences, gifts we could have no reason to expect. Borges says: "Music, states of happiness, mythology, faces belaboured by time, certain twilights and certain places try to tell us something, or have said something we should have missed, or are about to say something; this imminence of a revelation which does not occur is, perhaps, the aesthetic phenomenon."[21] Despite Hegel's claim that philosophy, not art, embodies the most serious aspirations, the autonomous work of art holds out the possibility that art may be one of the forms in which the world is transfigured. The work of art is sustained by the different form of attention it provokes; different especially from the passivity with which most instances of popular or dependent art are received; different, too, from the kind of attention that dissolves a work of art into its subject matter. So far as it is autonomous, a work of art is "inexhaustible to meditation." Further: the autonomous work of art is opposed not only to the conditions which produce dependent art but to the conditions—often the same ones—which have provoked its own autonomy. The work must take its chances in a society largely but not entirely given over to entertainment and fashion: it is distinguishable from dependent art, subject to the consideration that many people are willing to be promiscuous toward both kinds. They like Beethoven's last quartets and "A Hard Day's Night." Finally, it is well understood that the autonomous work of art may be subject to an impure motive. T. J. Clark finds such a motive even in the Abstract Expressionism he for the most part admires—the work of Adolph Gottlieb, Jackson Pollock, and Clifford Still: "Abstract Expressionism, I want to say, is the style of a certain petty bourgeoisie's aspiration to aristocracy, to a totalizing cultural power. It is the art of that moment when the petty bourgeoisie thinks it can speak (and its masters allow it to speak) the aristocrat's claim to individuality. Vulgarity is the form of that aspiration."[22]

So far, Kant's aesthetic and especially his description of disinterestedness seem to exempt us from political duty: the judgment of taste is contemplative, not cognitive. A judgment of taste, as a subjective principle, has no significance as knowledge. Aesthetic judgment is its own law. We seem to be given a sabbatical from our political duties, even allowing for Adorno's claim that the silence of disinterestedness speaks of the possibility of a better life. But Kant summons us back from our sabbatical when he presents a difficult account of nature and art. The difficulty has not always been recognized. John Crowe Ransom and those colleagues of his in the New Criticism who were philosophically inclined thought that Kant authorized them to take the autonomy of a poem for granted and to treat the question of nature and art as an easy one. Ransom thought that Kant allowed him to assume "natural piety" as a sufficient basis for his poetics: "The faith of Kant the philosopher was formed on intellectual grounds, it was other-worldly yet of extreme Protestant severity, quite declining to let the imagination of this world give it a form. I should say that we might call the poet's piety a 'natural' piety, his gift being for finding the natural world not merely mechanical but hospitable to the moral Universal."[23] But Ransom does not feel, as Adorno does, "the primordial shudder in the age of reification," terror in the presence of reified objects, the shudder "permanently reproduced in the historical antagonism of subject and object."[24] Kant's account of the relation between the beauty of nature and the beauty of a work of art is not as easy as Ransom implies. It appears from Kant that a work of art has only one merit over a scene in nature: that it is more directly a symbol of morality. Gadamer's commentary in *Truth and Method* makes this clearer than it is in Kant. When we find a scene in nature beautiful—the scene itself having no significance of content—we feel that nature has produced this beauty in our favor. Nature has given us a sign that we are the ultimate goal of creation. The sign speaks to us of our intelligible destiny. A work of art also speaks to us, but it exists only in order to address us in this way. That we encounter ourselves in a work of art does not mean that we are confirmed in our existence by another, or that another set of signs is addressing us: we are acknowledged only by ourselves.

Gadamer deals with this problem by saying that one advantage of a work of art over natural beauty is the fact "that the language of art is a demanding language which does not offer itself freely and vaguely for our interpretation according to one's mood, but speaks to us in a significant and definite way." And the remarkable thing about a work of art is that this definiteness, far from being a burden on our minds, opens for us "the area in which freedom operates in the play of our mental faculties."[25] Kant allows for this by saying that aesthetic ideas are free from conceptual determination and by celebrating the action of genius as the art of making the free play of the mental faculties communicable.[26] By confining genius to the artistically beautiful, he makes possible a philosophy of art as distinct from an appreciation of natural beauty.

But Kant's legacy in this regard is contentious, as commentaries by Foucault and later by Derrida have shown. Derrida has claimed that Kant's third *Critique* depends on a pragmatic anthropology and a reflective humanism. If the person who makes aesthetic judgments "is not recognized as an anthropological unity," and if the play of his functions—sensitivity, imagination, understanding, reason—is not bound "under the name of man occupying a privileged place in nature," then, according to Derrida, Kant's whole argument makes no sense. If, however, "a determined anthropology intervenes in this critique of aesthetic judgment," then "an entire theory of history, society, and culture decides the issue at what is formally the most critical moment."[27] The same case could be brought against Hegel's aesthetic: it is anthropomorphically prejudiced. There would appear to be no way out. Or if there is, it is by recognizing, within the terminology of genius, that the sublime is a mode of imagination which does not refute the beautiful but directs a force of perturbation through its forms.²⁸ In Kant, the sublime has nothing to do with art: it is a feeling in someone, provoked by an object in nature before which her imagination trembles, till her reason reasserts itself. Reason then feels exhilarated to discover that its rational and moral powers are still in command. It is fear, to begin with, till fear is replaced by a conviction of recovered rational power; as Lyotard puts it, "the pleasure that reason should exceed all presentation, the pain that imagination or sensibility should not be equal to the concept."²⁹ It is true, as Ernst Bloch remarks, that classical aesthetics, as in Kant and Schopenhauer, "restricts relations with the beautiful to pure contemplation and the beautiful itself to its purified forms."³⁰ But the contemplation is bound to be ill at ease, because it senses a perturbation in the scene, perhaps on the heights of the next mountain. The sublime makes the sense of beauty fear for its security, just as genius sends taste and pleasure into abeyance. In the sublime, the mind is beside itself; thinking defies its limits, forms stare into formlessness, and the aesthetic faculty shudders. It is best to think of these states of feeling as secular versions of religious experiences, peremptory intuitions of the holy, of mystical rapture, and of transcendence. The sublime transgresses grammar and syntax in its collusion with the unsayable: it is that for which the undiscursive arts—music, painting, sculpture, dance—were invented, words having been shown to be inadequate. What these experiences say about the "anthropological unity" and the "reflective humanism" that Derrida finds so disabling in Kant's third *Critique*, I'm not sure. It is possible to imagine these states of mind, which we associate with known limits and accepted forms, driven beyond themselves. If so, Derrida's analysis may not be as damaging as it seems. In the first Duino elegy, Rilke imagines angels in their overwhelming force of being, and makes beauty and terror alike transcendent: "If one of them suddenly took me to his heart," he writes, "I would perish from his powerful being, for the Beautiful is nothing but the onset of the Terror we can scarcely endure, and we are fascinated because it calmly disdains to obliterate us."[31] There is a comparable passage in *Middlemarch* where George Eliot writes: "If we had a keen vision and feeling of all ordinary human life, it would be like hearing the grass grow and the squirrel's heart beat, and we should die of that roar which lies on the other side of silence."[32] This sentence is itself sublime, because "die" and "roar" and "other" and "silence" are evidently unequal to whatever it is they are called upon to say. Yet the sentence recovers itself in its syntax.

Iris Murdoch argued that Kant's theory of beauty is weak in two respects. It represents the relation between subject and the object of attention as entirely contemplative rather than as a dynamic relation between one form of life and another; and it should have presented the theory of the sublime as a theory of tragedy. We should think of the spectator "not as gazing at the Alps, but at the spectacle of human life."[33]

But I should not imply that the aesthetic attitude and the definition of beauty depended entirely on Kant. There were several forces at work that eventually established beauty as a more or less independent value. Most of them involved the secularization or domestication of religious values: when the religious meaning was removed, nothing remained of the symbol but its secular form, which could be recognized as beautiful or not. Hogarth's *Columbus Breaking the Egg* is a travesty of the Last Supper: the Christian reference has no claim upon Hogarth, so those who look at the work are free to find it funny or even, if they wish, formally charming. They are not obliged to be pious in its presence. In *The Rape of the Lock* what was once a Christian cross has become a piece of jewelry on Belinda's bosom: you can find it beautiful if you are indifferent—as Pope is not—to its Christian purport.[34] Addison writes about the "beauties" of each Book of *Paradise Lost* while he ignores the theological and political bearing of the poem. In the same spirit you could refuse to be impressed by representations of gods and goddesses in classical sculpture and, like Hogarth, prefer the "living woman" to the most perfect antique Venus.[35]

When you remove from an object its historical, religious, or cultural claim, you make it available to be appreciated—or not—for its own sake: in practice this means for its attributes of form and texture.

III

The history of landscape architecture shows a similar development. John Dixon Hunt has documented the demand, in the middle and later years of the eighteenth century, for gardens expressive rather than emblematic. In an emblematic garden, particular cultural and political values are inscribed by means of carefully chosen statues, historical figures, and quoted legends. An expressive garden leaves one free to reflect or dream. Free, also, to appreciate the beauty of a garden that has no cultural design upon you. In 1740 Joseph Warton's poem "Enthusiast or the Lover of Nature" denounced "gardens deck'd with art's vain pomps." In 1770 Thomas Whately's *Observations on Modern Gardening* rejected the statues of gods, goddesses, and heroes, "columns erected only to receive quotations," and gardens filled with puerile allusions calling to be deciphered. Hunt gives several reasons for the advance of expressive gardens: a change in the patronage of architectural landscapists from aristocrats to less learned gentry and bourgeoisie; a movement of interest from Italian and French to Dutch art; a greater appreciation of British landscapes and artifacts—as by Edmund Bolton, who said of Stonehenge: "The dumbness of it . . . speaks"; the tendency of English travelers to find the Alps inspiring precisely because no emblematic message intimidated the experience of looking at them; and finally the influence of Locke's epistemology, which gave the individual mind power to shape its own experience.[36] The new garden did not obtrude upon one's sensibility: it allowed the mind to wander among its feelings and to appreciate the moments in which nature seemed to gratify one's taste. In *Pride and Prejudice,* as Hunt remarks, Elizabeth Bennett changes from the woman who exclaimed "What are men to rocks and mountains?" to the more mature woman who appreciates the landscapes at Pemberley Woods and notes, in front of Mr. Darcy's Pemberley House, the stream "of some natural importance . . . swelled into greater, but without any artificial appearance. Its banks were neither formal, nor falsely adorned." Elizabeth, we are told, was delighted: "She had never seen a place for which nature had done more, or where natural beauty had been so little counteracted by an awkward taste."[37] Her appreciation of Pemberley's owner will develop from the same considerations.

The change from emblematic gardening to expressive gardening entailed the removal of cultural artifacts, deemed to be intrusive. What they intruded upon was the natural scene — or the scene fancied to be natural — and the free movement of one's feelings. One's sense of beauty did not turn away from cultural artifacts as such, but from artifacts regarded as foreign and culturally intimidating. Travelers had no choice. If you wanted to appreciate the beauty of Venice, you had to go to Venice. The beauty of the Blue Mosque, Mary's church at Chartres, the Dome of the Rock, and Matisse's windows in the chapel at Vence can be appreciated only in relation to the religious values these buildings embody or once embodied. But the discourse of beauty was greatly developed and clarified by a consideration of objects that had been removed from their original settings. It was easier to think of their beauty as autonomous now that they no longer served a cultural or religious purpose. The Elgin Marbles were a case in point.

In *Reading Public Romanticism* Paul Magnuson has studied the debate that followed when it was proposed that the British government should buy Lord Elgin's statues on behalf of the nation. Most of the prominent artists and critics were called to give evidence before the Select Committee of the House of Commons early in 1816. They were specifically asked to say how the statues would survive comparison with the Apollo Belvedere and the Laocoön. In public debate or before the Select Committee, Flaxman and Richard Payne Knight maintained that the marbles were inferior to those masterpieces; Haydon, Canova, Hazlitt, Sir Thomas Lawrence, and Benjamin West thought the marbles superior to any other comparable sculptures. The debate soon turned into a dispute between those followers of Sir Joshua Reynolds, who held that sculpture should present ideal figures, and those radicals, as we may call them, who insisted that great sculptures must be drawn, as the Elgin Marbles evidently were, from the life. Hazlitt praised them in these terms: "[They possess] no alliteration or antithesis . . . , no setness, squareness, affectation or formality of appearance. The different muscles do not present a succession of *tumuli*, each heaving with big throes to rival the other. If one is raised, the other falls quietly into its place." [38] Reynolds's followers spoke up for the classical tradition, the grandeur of ideal generality, and systematic art. Their opponents appealed rather to the creative imagination and the inspiring force of nature, and in their extreme statements dissented not only from Reynolds but from Kant. "What the imagination seizes as Beauty must be truth—whether it existed before or not," Keats told Benjamin Bailey in a letter of November 22, 1817. [39] In "Ode on a Grecian Urn" the urn is a pure form, removed from its first use. What it says is prophetic rather than descriptive. It is as if the urn, now that it has been removed from its historical setting, can speak of a time when Beauty and Truth will be one and the same because they will alike and equally be products of the imagination. This "time" is anticipated by the experiences of reading, writing, and remembering.

Hazlitt and Keats saw most clearly the significance of the Elgin Marbles for the theory of beauty. In a general comment Hazlitt remarked:

> History, as well as religion, has contributed to enlarge the bounds of imagination; and both together, by showing past and future objects at an interminable distance, have accustomed the mind to contemplate and take an interest in the obscure and shadowy. . . . The mere lapse of time then, aided by the art of printing, has served to accumulate for us an endless mass of mixed and contradictory materials; and, by extending our knowledge to a greater number of things, has made our particular ideas less perfect and distinct . . . We are lost in wonder at what has been done, and dare not think of emulating it.[40]

Hazlitt means that we can now take an aesthetic interest in objects so numerous, so mixed, and so far removed from their historical and religious meanings. But he also claims that this experience offers a further range of the beautiful. As Keats wrote in his sonnet "On Seeing the Elgin Marbles":

> My spirit is too weak; mortality
> > Weighs heavily on me like unwilling sleep,
> > And each imagined pinnacle and steep
> Of godlike hardship tells me I must die
> Like a sick eagle looking at the sky.
> > Yet 'tis a gentle luxury to weep,

That I have not the cloudy winds to keep
Fresh for the opening of the morning's eye.
Such dim-conceived glories of the brain
    Bring round the heart an indescribable feud;
So do these wonders a most dizzy pain,
    That mingles Grecian grandeur with the rude
Wasting of old Time—with a billowy main,
    A sun, a shadow of a magnitude.[41]

Keats seems to say that a sense of endless cultural distance, going along with not knowing precisely what in the marbles he is looking at, has given him a domestic variant of the sublime. If one of the constituents of the sublime was the colossal, what he apprehends is a "shadow of a magnitude." Hazlitt expressed a similar relation to the marbles. Now that they have been removed from their first setting and he knows virtually nothing about them, he is free to look at them without feeling culturally burdened:

> Nothing remains of them but their style; but that is everything, for it is the style of nature. Art is the imitation of nature; and the Elgin Marbles are in their essence and their perfection casts from nature, —from fine nature, it is true, but from real, living, moving nature; from objects in nature, answering to an idea in the artist's mind, not from an idea in the artist's mind abstracted from all objects in nature.[42]

Hazlitt is not saying that an object must be released from its first setting to be appreciated for its beauty. But he seems to be saying that where we have an object removed in this way, there may be a cultural loss, but there is also the gain of having a new relation to the object. Emerson thought the Elgin Marbles badly arranged—"a warehouse of old marbles," he called them. But he sensed the new experience of their beauty that Hazlitt adumbrated: "People go to the Elgin chamber many times & at last the beauty of the whole comes to them at once like music. The figures sit like gods in heaven."[43] The new relation is spontaneously aesthetic—"at once like music." Under its direction we cheerfully grant the object a new quality, autonomy—which corresponds to our disinterestedness. Autonomy, disinterestedness, and impersonality are the values to be recognized; especially in Keats's poetry, where in such poems as "To Autumn" and "Ode on a Grecian Urn" he seeks impersonality more avowedly than any other Romantic poet. In that respect, Hazlitt and Keats are at one. Each wants the object to be available, impersonally, by being apprehended aesthetically. Hazlitt and Emerson do not go as far as Nietzsche goes in that direction. They do not release themselves from the entire burden of the past by saying, as Nietzsche does in "The Use and Abuse of History," that we seek a past from which we may spring, rather than that past from which we appear to have derived. But the differences between Hazlitt, Emerson, and Nietzsche on this point are only differences of degree.

IV

The attitude I'm referring to is still available. In *Aesthetic Theory* Adorno writes of the relation between the beautiful and the ugly:

> Nietzsche's dictum that all good things were once dreadful things, like Schelling's insight into the terror of the beginning, may well have had their origins in the experience of art. The overthrown and recurrent content (*Inhalt*) is sublimated in imagination and form. Beauty is not the platonically pure beginning but rather something that originated in the

renunciation of what was once feared, which only
as a result of this renunciation—retrospectively, so
to speak, according to its own telos—became the
ugly.[44]

Sublimation, as Adorno thinks of it, seems to correspond in the
artist to disinterestedness in the viewer and autonomy in the
work of art. Under any of these terms, the claims exerted by the
past and its rigmarole are set aside as if they were obstacles—
as indeed they are—to the discovery of artistic form. Adorno's
aesthetic theory never moves away from fear and the devices for
overcoming it: "The image of beauty as that of a single and dif-
ferentiated something originates with the emancipation from
the fear of the overpowering wholeness and undifferentiated-
ness of nature. The shudder in the face of this is rescued by
beauty into itself by making itself impervious to the immediately existent; beauty establishes a sphere of untouchability."[45]
But Adorno doesn't hesitate to say that the imagination that
sublimes undifferentiated nature into form has cruelty among
its attributes: "In aesthetic forms, cruelty becomes imagination:
Something is excised from the living, from the body of language,
from tones, from visual experience. The purer the form and the
higher the autonomy of the works, the more cruel they are."[46]
There is no merit, I agree, in claiming that the creative imagination is innocent. When R. P. Blackmur presented the idio-
syncrasy of Marianne Moore's sensibility as constituting "the
perfection of standing aside," he knew that a price must be paid
for this perfection, either as a defect somewhere else in Moore's
poetry or a limitation throughout.[47] But it is a saving if not a
decisive grace in art that the cruel work of sublimation can only
seem to be successful. There is always a residue of undifferentiated matter, despite every effort on the artist's part to sublime it
away. And there are artists who hold it as a matter of conscience

to respect the materiality of nature and the world and to see that it is not entirely sublimated or transcended.

Levinas was troubled by the most elementary procedure of art, as it appeared to him, that it replaces the object by its image and neutralizes what would otherwise be a "living relationship with a real object."[48] The most insidious temptation an artist faces, according to Levinas, is "fusion":

> One begins with the idea that duality must be transformed into unity, and that social relations must culminate in communion. This is the last vestige of a conception that identifies being with knowledge, that is, with the event through which the multiplicity of reality ends up referring to a single being and where, through the miracle of clarity, everything that encounters me exists as coming from me. It is the last vestige of idealism.[49]

But Levinas recognized that some artists resist that temptation; notably Proust, who situates reality in a relation with something which forever remains itself, absent, mysterious, exempt from sublimation.[50] It is as if the cruelty that Adorno ascribed to the imagination rebuked itself and tried to make amends in newly chastened forms of beauty.

These references to Adorno and Levinas are perhaps enough to indicate that beauty and the aesthetic sense are to be thought of in difficult contexts and relations. Adorno's *Aesthetic Theory*, in particular, has shown that "the beautiful is no more to be defined than its concept can be dispensed with."[51] But there are other difficulties. One of them is a modern repetition of Baumgarten's insistence on subjecting the beautiful to rational principles. Nelson Goodman's *Languages of Art* holds that "aesthetic experience is cognitive experience" and should be "judged by standards of cognitive efficacy."[52] I associate this attitude with the determination, common since the rise of Structuralism, to submit every experience to concepts and codes. The standard rejection of "genius" as a term in literary criticism comes from the same explanatory zeal, though I have no idea what other concept would respond to the work of Shakespeare, Blake, Beethoven, Dickinson, or any other great artist. As Michel Serres has remarked, "You can always proceed from the product to its conditions, but never from the conditions to the product."[53] There is always an incalculable factor, whether we call it genius or something else.

Another problem, nobody's fault, is the question of aesthetic distance, not the historical distance that Hazlitt pondered but the distance that must be kept if the beautiful is to be appreciated. In "Certain Noble Plays of Japan" Yeats says that "all imaginative art remains at a distance and this distance, once chosen, must be firmly held against a pushing world."[54] There is no harm in that or in Yeats's preferring a Noh play to a realistic novel. But it becomes an awkward claim when we read this passage from Tim O'Brien's *The Things They Carried:*

> The truths are contradictory. It can be argued, for instance, that war is grotesque. But in truth war is also beauty. For all its horror, you can't help but gape at the awful majesty of combat. You stare out at tracer rounds unwinding through the dark like brilliant red ribbons. You crouch in ambush as a cool, impassive moon rises over the nighttime paddies. You admire the fluid symmetries of troops on the move, the harmonies of sound and shape and proportion, the great sheets of metal-fire streaming down from a gun-ship, the illumination rounds, the white phosphorus, the purply orange glow of napalm, the rocket's red glare. It's not pretty, exactly.

It's astonishing. It fills the eye. It commands you.
You hate it, yes, but your eyes do not.[55]

O'Brien is not writing an editorial or a warmonger's manifesto; the sentiments he expresses are ascribed to one of his characters in the novel; they are not necessarily his own. But it is hard to separate the sensibility at work in this passage from the cruelty of imagination to which Adorno refers unless you decide that the speaker's personality is woefully split or his moral sense inert. The terms of praise are the standard ones in a major tradition of aesthetics: beauty, symmetry, harmony, shape, proportion. "You hate it, but your eyes do not." No wonder Fredric Jameson argues that "the visible is *essentially* pornographic, which is to say that it has its end in rapt, mindless fascination."[56]

Good causes are regularly damaged by exorbitant claims for them, and by excesses in their practice; as by Nietzsche's hyperbole, that "the existence of the world is justified only as an aesthetic phenomenon."[57] The good cause, in this case, is the beautiful, which can be apprehended only by standing aside from a pushing world. Politically, this amounts to a form of pacifism as critique, to be practiced for the time being. It is critique because images of the beautiful can shame a society out of its self-satisfaction, as Walker Evans's photographs for the Farm Security Administration in the 1930s showed that beauty of feature was not confined to the well-off classes. The attitude is like the one that Marianne Moore expressed in her poem "In Distrust of Merits," where she meditated on the causes of war and, finding her way with the aid of rhyming monosyllables—dust, must, trust—ended with this stanza:

> Hate-hardened heart, O heart of iron,
> iron is iron till it is rust.
> There never was a war that was
> not inward; I must

fight till I have conquered in myself what
causes war, but I would not believe it.
I inwardly did nothing.
    O Iscariot-like crime!
Beauty is everlasting
    And dust is for a time.[58]

She probably means beauty as humanity, universal acknowledgment of human beings. I find no harm in that nearly pacifist
sentiment. The pushing world will win soon enough. But meanwhile I think of another problem, that apprehension of the beautiful requires an active sense of the intrinsic, the gratuitous, respect for things in themselves and for their own sake. It is not a
common cultural practice, and it has to defend itself against the
other rhetoric, the one that demands that practices be seen to be
useful. The humanities are always being asked to be applicable
or to consider themselves luxuries that society may choose not
to maintain.

What then is the status—including the political status—of
the beautiful? It has just as strong a case for consideration as
the true and the good. No formula for this consideration comes
to my mind, not even the merit of dissent, which I regard in
general as the best available stance. But it seems clear that the
"tense" of beauty is the future, and that its apprehension is pro-
pelled by a politics of hope and anticipation, a surge of feeling beyond the merely given present moment. Bloch's *Spirit of
Utopia* and *Principle of Hope* provide incitement in the theory
of this enterprise, which is largely predicated on music as "the
inwardly utopian art."[59] Bloch offers a program for art when he
proposes as "the criterion of purely aesthetic illumination, considered in terms of its ultimate categories: how could things be
consummated, without apocalyptically ceasing to be."[60] Stendhal said that beauty "is only the promise of happiness."[61] It is not

even so much; but it is a figure of happiness, not a promise but a hint of possibility. The criterion is elaborated in *The Principle of Hope*, where beauty and even sublimity represent an existence for objects "which has not yet become"; a "thoroughly formed world, without external chance; without the inessential, the unrendered."[62] At any moment there is by definition no such place, it depends for its realization on the combined forces of desire, hope, and imagination. In *Defense of Poetry* Shelley anticipates Bloch by speaking of poets as the mirrors of the gigantic shadows which futurity casts upon the present.

Henry James called the place of hope "the country of the blue," as if it anticipated the fulfillment of every desire of the imagination. In "The Next Time" he tells of Ray Limbert, a writer of exquisite failures, doomed to write novels at a time of "trash triumphant." Every year he tries to write a popular adventure story in the hope of supporting his wife and their several children, but every year he turns out a great performance rather than a great success. He cannot write anything but irrepressible works of art, beautiful and therefore disregarded by the lending-library public. Ill and suffering every privation, he gets an idea for a novel to be called *Derogation*. But this time he is so far sunk in privations that he cannot lift himself even for the sake of being popular. The narrator divines that Limbert "had floated away into a grand indifference, into a reckless consciousness of art":

> What had happened, I was afterwards satisfied, was that he had quite forgotten whether he generally sold or not. He had merely waked up one morning again in the country of the blue and had stayed there with a good conscience and a great idea. He stayed till death knocked at the gate, for the pen dropped from his hand only at the moment when from sud-

den failure of the heart his eyes, as he sank back in his chair, closed for ever. *Derogation* is a splendid fragment; it evidently would have been one of his high successes. I am not prepared to say it would have waked up the libraries.[63]

I interpret the country of the blue as the place of the imagination where it has nothing at heart but to be inventive and intelligent and to live up to its best possibility; where it has checked its ordinary cruelty and determined to add another beautiful thing to the world. It is blue because the sky is blue or it returns to blue after having been yellow or black or pale or hectic red; or because deep lakes and oceans are blue. If it is blue like the sky, it is also endless and immune to the abrasion of other countries. Blue is the freedom in which Ray Limbert eventually works rather than the character otherwise of what he writes. There is no reason to think his freedom absolute, but—like Stevens's "man with the blue guitar"—it is sufficient for the most demanding art and the beauty it may attain. I assume that the main quality of Ray Limbert's writing is transparency and that it derogates from all the vulgar temptations in its path.

3

Every Wrinkle the Touch of a Master

I

When we say that beauty is a value—"a species of value," as Santayana puts it—we do not necessarily decide whether it is to be ascribed to the world or to ourselves. It may be "an emotional element, a pleasure of ours, which nevertheless we regard as a quality of things."[1] It seems to me a quality of things at least in the sense that without the things one's sense of beauty would have no occasion to be activated. But even if we can't resolve this theoretical issue, we can say that every such occasion must be interpreted, dealt with as a constituent or a practice of the general culture, one of many. Interpretation brings into the social world the object or the event to which it pays attention, and offers it to be admired. And, in many cases, to be bought. There is no merit in being dainty about such processes. Museums, art galleries, and concert halls are estimable institutions, but they are not exempt from the aims of publicity, advertising, fashion, and the market. Andrea Bocelli has a beautiful voice: he is also an immensely valuable property to be bought and sold, just as much as Andre Agassi. Society and the social classes are also cultural institutions in which beautiful objects, many of them women, are put on display and sometimes offered for what amounts to sale. Among the novelists, Henry James was especially alert to the little dramas of beauty, not only in the major novels but in short stories. "The Beldonald Holbein" seems to me one of the most perceptive stories of the social provenance of beauty.

The scene is London at the end of the nineteenth century.

The narrator, whose name we do not know, is an artist, a painter well regarded by the Academy. One day he is approached by a friend, Mrs. Munden, with a suggestion that he do a portrait of her sister-in-law, Lady Beldonald. Nina Beldonald is a widow and an American, two attributes that may amount to a complication for her in London society though they are not in principle a liability. She is also regarded as a beauty. But in Mrs. Munden's opinion, Lady Beldonald has not—or not yet—put herself forward in society in the ways a great beauty should. She has not done what such a person ought to do, and in her failure or passivity she is getting on Mrs. Munden's nerves. It is implied, but never asserted, that Nina has not used her beauty with a view to being taken up by an eligible man in want of a beautiful wife. If a portrait of her by a well-regarded painter were to be shown at the Academy's exhibition next season, it might have the effect of bringing her forward. The painter takes on the assignment and arranges a preliminary meeting with Lady Beldonald. After the meeting, he decides that her beauty begins and ends with her appearance:

> . . . and then I understood that her life had its center in her own idea of her appearance. Nothing else about her mattered—one knew her all when one knew that. She is indeed in one particular, I think, sole of her kind—a person whom vanity has had the odd effect of keeping positively safe and sound. This passion is supposed surely, for the most part, to be a principle of perversion and injury, leading astray those who listen to it and landing them, sooner or later, in this or that complication; but it has landed her ladyship nowhere whatever—it has kept her from the first moment of full consciousness, one feels, exactly in the same place.[2]

Lady Beldonald does not speak of these considerations. We hear nothing of any disappointments she may have or of her failure to replace a dead husband with a live one. Presumably she thinks so well of her beauty that no man, even a healthy and rich one, could be seriously thought of for her favor. We infer such a sentiment from the degree to which she gets on Mrs. Munden's nerves. But Lady Beldonald does not assume that her appearance will be appreciated without doing anything in its favor. She employs, as a foil to her beauty, a companion—Miss Dadd—who is universally held to be plain. Miss Dadd deals with the servants, keeps the accounts, makes the tea, and arranges the light, but her first duty to the beautiful Lady Beldonald is to be plain, and her second is never to rise above herself. It is awkward that Miss Dadd is ill and soon dies. Lady Beldonald must replace her. She chooses a kinswoman of her own, Mrs. Brash, who is widowed and not at all comfortably off. She lives in America, but at the age of fifty-seven she is ready to remove herself to London. She has the merit of being, like Miss Dadd, plain to the degree of being ugly.

It happens that the narrator arranges a small afternoon party and invites Lady Beldonald, Mrs. Brash, and a number of other guests, most of them young. The occasion is the visit to London of a French painter, Paul Outreau, a friend of the narrator's. Half an hour or so after the party has begun, Outreau says to his host: "Bonté divine, mon cher—que cette vieille est donc belle!" The host assumes that the reference is to Lady Beldonald, and he protests that while not in her first youth she could not justly be called old. But it turns out that Outreau is referring to Mrs. Brash: "She's the greatest of all the great Holbeins." The narrator looks at her and sees that she is indeed a Holbein, and that he must paint her portrait: "It was before me with intensity, in the light of Mrs. Brash's distant perfection of a little white old face, in which every wrinkle was the touch of a master."[3] Impulsively, he makes the blunder of telling Lady Beldonald that her companion is a true Holbein, "the wonderful sharp old face—so extraordinarily, consummately drawn—in the frame of dark velvet." Lady Beldonald is appalled that he should even think of painting Mrs. Brash's portrait. The narrator is slow to recognize the beginning of a complication. "She brings the old boy to life!" he exclaims to Lady Beldonald. "It's just as I should call you a Titian. You bring *him* to life." Lady Beldonald is not assuaged, and protests to the narrator that Mrs. Brash has never been thought to be anything but plain:

> "Don't you understand that she has always been supposed ——?" It had the ring of impatience; nevertheless, on a scruple, it stopped short.
>
> I knew what it was, however, well enough to say it for her if she preferred. "To be nothing whatever to look at? To be unfortunately plain—or even if you like repulsively ugly? Oh yes, I understand it perfectly, just as I understand—I have to as a part of my trade—many other forms of stupidity. It's nothing new to one that ninety-nine people out of a hundred have no eyes, no sense, no taste. There are whole communities impenetrably sealed. I don't say your friend is a person to make the men turn round in Regent Street. But it adds to the joy of the few who do see that they have it so much to themselves."[4]

Lady Beldonald refuses to have her portrait done by the narrator. Mrs. Brash, too, refuses, but for a different reason: "it was quite enough for her," she tells the painter, "that I had with that fine precipitation invited her." She acknowledges that "I would have painted her beautifully if she hadn't prevented me." But the damage between Lady Beldonald and Mrs. Brash, as between

Lady Beldonald and the painter, is done. The painter and Mrs. Munden know that they have taken on a responsibility, but he exults in it: "We can do this: we can give to a harmless and sensitive creature hitherto practically disinherited—and give with an unexpectedness that will immensely add to its price—the pure joy of a deep draft of the very pride of life, of an acclaimed personal triumph, in our superior, sophisticated world."[5] Mrs. Munden exclaims: "Oh, it will be beautiful!" In no time, the word goes round in the painter's little set, "bounded on the north by Ibsen and on the south by Sargent," that there is a Holbein in their company and that her name is Mrs. Brash. Soon Mrs. Brash allows the thought to enter her mind that she may have a face. She is transformed, not least in her own eyes: "Her whole nature had been pitched in the key of her supposed plainness. She had known how to be ugly—it was the only thing she had learnt save, if possible, how not to mind it. Being beautiful, at any rate, took a new set of muscles."[6] The painter says to Mrs. Munden: "It took but a few moments—but she tasted of the tree." Not that he has played the serpent and tempted Mrs. Brash, but the consequence is the same: she will never again be free of knowledge. Not of the knowledge of good and evil; that is not the form in which it arises. Tasting of the tree has the modern consequence of self-consciousness. Emerson is its philosopher, as in "Experience": "It is very unhappy, but too late to be helped, the discovery we have made that we exist. That discovery is called the Fall of Man. Ever afterwards we suspect our instruments. We have learned that we do not see directly, but mediately, and that we have no means of correcting these colored and distorting lenses which we are, or of computing the amount of their errors."[7] Socially, Mrs. Brash becomes a triumph, her "wonderful little career" was "in our particular circle one of the features of the following season." She was "practically enthroned and surrounded and more or less mobbed" as the "famous Holbein."

Lady Beldonald deals with the situation as graciously as she can: "She took our friend out, she showed her at home, never attempted to hide or to betray her, played her no trick whatever so long as the ordeal lasted. She drank deep, on *her* side too, of the cup—the cup that for her own lips could only be bitterness. There was, I think, scarce a special success of her companion's at which she was not personally present."[8] Lady Beldonald even pretends—or convinces herself—that she knows what a Holbein is and that Mrs. Brash is one. But after a few painful months she can't stand the situation any longer, dismisses Mrs. Brash, and sends her back to America. She replaces her with a young woman who was "as little a Holbein, or a specimen of any other school, as she was, like Lady Beldonald herself, a Titian." She is merely pretty:

> The formula was easy to give, for the amusement was that her prettiness—yes, literally, prodigiously, her prettiness—was distinct. Lady Beldonald had been magnificent—had been almost intelligent. Miss What's-her-name continues pretty, continues even young, and doesn't matter a straw! She matters so ideally little that Lady Beldonald is practically safer, I judge, than she has ever been. There has not been a symptom of chatter about this person, and I believe her protectress is much surprised that we are not more struck.[9]

Lady Beldonald tells the painter that she is now willing to sit for her portrait. He is no longer enthusiastic, but he supposes that he will take up the delayed commission. As for Mrs. Brash:

> Mrs. Munden remained in correspondence with Mrs. Brash—to the extent, that is, of three letters, each of which she showed me. They so told, to our

imagination, her terrible little story that we were
quite prepared—or thought we were—for her going
out like a snuffed candle. She resisted, on her return to her original conditions, less than a year; the
taste of the tree, as I had called it, had been fatal to
her; what she had contentedly enough lived without before for half a century she couldn't now live
without for a day. I know nothing of her original
conditions—some minor American city—save that
for her to have gone back to them was clearly to
have stepped out of her frame. We performed, Mrs.
Munden and I, a small funeral service for her by
talking it all over and making it all out. It wasn't—
the minor American city—a market for Holbeins,
and what had occurred was that the poor old picture, banished from its museum and refreshed by the
rise of no new movement to hang it, was capable of
the miracle of a silent revolution, of itself turning,
in its dire dishonour, its face to the wall. So it stood,
without the intervention of a ghost of a critic, till
they happened to pull it round again and find it mere
dead paint.[10]

The story ends ambiguously. The painter reflects that he has not
the least note of Mrs. Brash, "not a scratch." Nothing remains
of the portrait but his first intention of painting it: "Mrs Munden continues to remind me, however, that this is not the sort
of rendering with which, on the other side, after all, Lady Beldonald proposes to content herself. She has come back to the
question of her own portrait. Let me settle it then at last. Since
she *will* have the real thing—well, hang it, she shall!"[11] What is
the real thing, the real Lady Beldonald? Is it a portrait of her as
a Titian, just as the portrait of Mrs. Brash would have presented

her as a Holbein? Will the painter paint her as the Titian she is not—not quite—or as a conventional beauty entirely without expression and merely the record of her preserved appearance? I interpret the real thing as the painter's revenge on Lady Beldonald for what she has done to Mrs. Brash. He will show her as she is, empty, expressionless, merely preserved.

II

But this is misleading. "He will show her as she is." I seem to have forgotten Emerson. In the late-nineteenth century there were three axioms of seeing. The first, which served well enough the aims of ontology, photography, politics, education, trade, empire-building, and the realistic novel, may be quoted from Matthew Arnold. In "On Translating Homer" (1862) and "The Function of Criticism at the Present Time" (1864) he wrote: "Of the literature of France and Germany, as of the intellect of Europe in general, the main effort, for now many years, has been a critical effort; the endeavour, in all branches of knowledge, theology, philosophy, history, art, science, to see the object as in itself it really is."[12] This, too, is Emersonian. Emerson does not doubt that objects are there: the only problem is that our self-consciousness, the modern version of Adam's curse, gets in the way of our seeing them. There is error, and we have no means of computing the nature and extent of it and allowing for correction. Arnold thought our cognitive instruments accurate enough for their needs, but he did not think their accuracy self-evident: the insistence of "in itself" and "really" concedes the difficulty. Still, if you concentrated on the object, you saw it, with that effort, as it really was, or as it appeared sufficiently for most purposes. It was no more difficult to see qualities than the objects on which they presented themselves. You could say that a particular chair was beautiful just as surely as that it was a chair.

The second axiom is available in Walter Pater. In his preface to *Studies in the History of the Renaissance* (1873) he pretended to take Arnold's formula devoutly, but he immediately turned away from it: "'To see the object as in itself it really is,' has been justly said to be the aim of all true criticism whatever; and in aesthetic criticism the first step towards seeing one's object as it really is, is to know one's own impression as it really is, to discriminate it, to realize it distinctly."[13] "Justly" is diplomatic talk; Pater doesn't believe it. "And" would have been "but" if he had been willing to make his disagreement with Arnold more explicit. The reference to "aesthetic criticism" was designed to separate Pater from Arnold, since Arnold was chiefly in Pater's eyes a social and political critic. The first step in the aesthetic criticism that Pater referred to was the only one he intended taking. Within a sentence, "one's own impression" dislodges "one's object" and becomes itself an object, the only one we can hope to know. Pater does not offer any evidence for thinking that the self-evident character of one's own impression is stronger than that of apparently external objects. He maintains the privilege of "impression" while using Arnoldian verbs to enforce it: "know," "discriminate," and "realize." These verbs are inevitable if you speak of knowledge and the content of knowledge. Santayana makes the point: "Even the knowledge of truth, which the most sober theologians made the essence of the beatific vision, is an aesthetic delight; for when the truth has no further practical utility, it becomes a landscape."[14] As an amateur psychologist of beauty, Pater needed, but did not have, a vocabulary of event, action, and motion. Without it, he could not avoid using the old terminology of subject and object, even while taking pleasure in the triumph of psychology over ontology. "Impression" was the most subjective word he could find, and it had the merit of pointing to a value as high in psychology, Romantic poetry, and Symbolism as in French painting.

It follows that a great critic according to Pater's way of seeing and knowing has a great sensibility, a temperament acutely susceptible to beautiful objects and attentive to the impressions they produce in him. Separating himself from Ruskin now, Pater says: "What is important, then, is not that the critic should possess a correct abstract definition of beauty for the intellect, but a certain kind of temperament, the power of being deeply moved by the presence of beautiful objects. He will remember always that beauty exists in many forms. To him all periods, types, schools of taste, are in themselves equal."[15] To the aesthetic critic, "the picture, the landscape, the engaging personality in life or in a book, *La Gioconda*, the hills of Carrara, Pico of Mirandola, are valuable for their virtues, as we say, in speaking of a herb, a wine, a gem; for the property each has of affecting one with a special, a unique, impression of pleasure." The aim of the aesthetic critic is to distinguish the virtue, in each case, on the authority of the particular impression it has produced in him. So in pondering *La Gioconda*, Pater tries, sentence by susceptible sentence, to disengage the virtue, the special quality of the Lady Lisa's face:

> The presence that rose thus so strangely beside the waters, is expressive of what in the ways of a thousand years men had come to desire. Hers is the head upon which all "the ends of the world are come," and the eyelids are a little weary. It is a beauty wrought out from within upon the flesh, the deposit, little cell by cell, of strange thoughts and fantastic reveries and exquisite passions. Set it for a moment beside one of those white Greek goddesses or beautiful women of antiquity, and how would they be troubled by this beauty, into which the soul with all its maladies has passed![16]

The whole passage, including sentences more famous than these, is Pater's formula—to use one of his favorite words—ostensibly for Leonardo's painting but really for the impression it has provoked in Pater's temperament. The formal properties of the painting are not examined. No attempt is made to separate the seen thing from the mind that has seen it. The seeing gathers to itself everything seen, retains the essence of it, and makes it an extension of the critic's sensibility. The unique impression of pleasure is conveyed in the diction, syntax, and movement of Pater's sentences, the murmuring of word upon word before the subject of a sentence reaches its verb or verb its object, the turning aside—as in the quotation from the first Corinthians—to gather up more of human experience, the final exclamation sinking to rest upon a general reflection, "the soul with all its maladies."

The third axiom is an extreme version of Pater's, a histrionic conceit in Oscar Wilde and a sociological observation in Jules de Gaultier. "The primary aim of the critic," according to Wilde, "is to see the object as in itself it really is not." "To the critic, the work of art is simply a suggestion for a new work of his own, that need not bear any obvious resemblance to the thing it criticizes."[17] We should reject, in favor of the deliverances of our own imaginations, the privilege conventionally given to nature, objects, facts, and truths, and the culture that sustains its vulgarity on that privilege. In *Bovarysm* de Gaultier maintains that this is what people are doing anyway; seeing themselves as they really are not. Emma Bovary is a typical victim of the habit: she chooses models from trashy fiction and lives by imitating their longings. In *Mensonge romantique et vérité romanesque*, René Girard develops this motif from de Gaultier and Max Scheler into a structuralist theory of "triangular desire," desire on the model of someone else rather than on one's own authority, which is what we regularly claim for ourselves. We insist that our feelings and desires are our own, spontaneous. But if de Gaultier and Girard are right, what we feel is not spontaneous but mediated desire; the mediation is effected, without our being aware of it, through others—rivals, archetypes, models, historical figures, styles. T. S. Eliot thought Othello a prime instance of Bovarysm, determined in his last speeches to see himself as he is not. With Emerson, we see not directly but mediately, but we do not know that we do. Our culture conspires with us in the delusion that our feelings are entirely our own and to be cherished for that reason.

"The Beldonald Holbein" seems to offer a fourth way of seeing, a variant of triangular desire which might be called triangular appreciation. Or *seeing as* rather than *seeing*. Paul Outreau, on first seeing Louisa Brash, is exempt from the conventional view that she is plain. He sees her as a Holbein, an exemplar of that genre. Presumably he sees her in the canonical company of Lady Margaret Butts, Anne of Cleves, Holbein's wife, and the other women whom Holbein drew or painted. He does not raise the question: without Holbein, would Mrs. Brash be beautiful, or would she be the plain woman she is generally held to be? In many of Holbein's portraits the women are beautiful subject to the consideration that they are plain, a situation hard to comprehend except by saying that in his art it is sufficient for a woman to be beautiful by being somehow interesting, full of expression, perhaps care-laden, time-worn or for some other reason taking one's attention. Outreau is free to see Mrs. Brash as a Holbein because he is an artist and, better still for his freedom, a French artist. His seeing her as a Holbein is not merely a description, it is an evaluation. To be a Holbein is to manifest a distinctive type of beauty without having to be a Titian. Outreau passes along this evaluation to his host, who accepts it at once: he, too, is an artist, though a merely English one. He might be expected to be afflicted with the standard idea of beauty in his society, according to which it might be easy to see Nina Beldonald as a Titian or a Sargent but not easy to see Louisa Brash as anything but plain. The narrator offers Outreau's evaluation of Louisa Brash, and his own, to Mrs. Munden, who is intelligent enough to see the justice of it. One word in a London drawing room leads to another, and before the season is out, Louisa is established as a Holbein. Presumably outside the drawing rooms and studios she is still seen, if seen at all, as not worth looking at, plain Mrs. Brash, but that doesn't matter. Once she herself accepts the attribution, she is as strongly in her Holbein frame as Nina Beldonald is in her Titian: more strongly, indeed. The domestic tragedy follows and is completed in the minor American city to which Louisa brings her transformed sense of herself.

I have referred to triangular appreciation, not triangular desire. Outreau and the narrator do not desire Louisa Brash, even though they think well enough of her appearance to judge her a Holbein. In that respect, they are disinterested. Kant could not ask for a purer form of attention. But in another respect they are impure. They take satisfaction in establishing Mrs. Brash as a Holbein, an object of social awe, and they are conscious of their superiority of taste and discrimination in doing so. "But it adds to the joy of the few who do see that they have it so much to themselves." Every connoisseur is a snob in favor of his acquisitions, but there is a point at which one's distaste for Outreau and the narrator should question itself. These men and Mrs. Munden are rapt in appreciation. There is no merit in asking whether they are simply mistaken about Louisa Brash's beauty. They see her as a Holbein, that is, not as a beauty in the general understanding but as a beauty according to Holbein's peculiar, well-established kind. The particular virtue—in Pater's sense of the word—of Holbein's paintings is the one that Outreau sees again in Mrs. Brash. "She's the greatest of all the great Holbeins," he tells the narrator in an outburst we have no grounds for calling exaggeration or hyperbole. There is no quarreling with his way of seeing or of speaking. Outreau and the narrator are competent witnesses. If they see Mrs. Brash as a Holbein, and declare her to be so, she is a Holbein to anyone who accepts the designation on her behalf. The only question is: will they persuade anyone else? Of course Holbein did not paint her, even though the narrator claims that "she was a good, hard, sixteenth-century figure, not withered with innocence, bleached rather by life in the open." He is even willing to concede that "her wonderful points must have been points largely the fruit of time."[18] But time, life, and Holbein are in league to define a certain style, a distinctive way of being in the world. No definition of beauty should exclude it. The history of art is the record of the innumerable ways of being beautiful, of appearing to qualified observers to be beautiful, and of seeing images as types of beauty. The history of art therefore limits the authority of the zeitgeist in saying what or who is beautiful: without it, we would have to take dictation in this matter from adepts of the fashion trade and other trades in its vicinity—advertising, cosmetics, Hollywood.

III

The history of art, and now of film, also allows us to make un-invidious distinctions, clarifying one instance of beauty by comparing it with another. The purpose of such comparisons is to appreciate differences without making the differentiations insolent. Roland Barthes's essay on Garbo, which glances at a comparison with Audrey Hepburn, is one of the happiest instances of such attention. Barthes maintains that Garbo, as in *Queen Christina*, belongs to "that moment in cinema when capturing the human face still plunged audiences into the deepest ecstasy," when the face represented "a kind of absolute state of the flesh, which could be neither reached nor renounced." "A few years earlier the face of Valentino was causing suicides; that of Garbo still partakes of the same rule of Courtly Love, where the flesh gives rise to mystical feelings of perdition."[19] Barthes does not say, as explicitly as I think Girard would, that Courtly Love is the mediator in one's desire for Garbo. Even those who have never heard of such love sense that their desire for Garbo can't be direct or spontaneous: not just because of the distancing force of the screen but because her beauty is such as not to permit intrusion. Ecstasy is permitted, "a consciousness of the world," as James Kirwan describes it, "so intense as to exclude our awareness that we are part of it."[20] But we are not allowed even the illusion of possession or the dream of touch. Barthes notes that in *Queen Christina* Garbo's makeup "has the snowy thickness of a mask: it is not a painted face, but one set in plaster, protected by the surface of the colour, not by its lineaments":

> Amid all this snow at once fragile and compact, the eyes alone, black like strange soft flesh, but not in the least expressive, are two faintly tremulous wounds. In spite of its extreme beauty, this face, not drawn but sculpted in something smooth and friable, that is, at once perfect and ephemeral, comes to resemble the flour-white complexion of Charlie Chaplin, the dark vegetation of his eyes, his totem-like countenance.[21]

Garbo offered to one's gaze "a sort of Platonic Idea of the human creature, which explains why her face is almost sexually undefined, without however leaving one in doubt." The name given to Garbo, "the Divine," "probably aimed to convey less a superlative state of beauty than the essence of her corporeal person, descended from a heaven where all things are formed and perfected in the clearest light."

Garbo knew this, as Barthes notes. I might add that her

knowing it does not convict her of egotism. She saw herself as a representative figure, not an assertive one: her beauty had only as much to do with her personally as was compatible with her being chosen by the gods to take up that exalted role. It might have happened to anyone. With the impersonal authority of a priestess, she tended her altar. Unlike other actresses, she would not allow the crowd to see her face change or its beauty mature: "The essence was not to be degraded, her face was not to have any reality except that of its perfection, which was intellectual even more than formal. The Essence became gradually obscured, progressively veiled with dark glasses, broad hats and exiles: but it never deteriorated." But it was not entirely a mask. There are hints of another destiny, though she will not complete it:

> And yet, in this deified face, something sharper than a mask is looming: a kind of voluntary and therefore human relation between the curve of the nostrils and the arch of the eyebrows; a rare, individual function relating two regions of the face. A mask is but a sum of lines; a face, on the contrary, is above all their thematic harmony. Garbo's face represents this fragile moment when the cinema is about to draw an existential from an essential beauty, when the archetype leans towards the fascination of mortal faces, when the clarity of the flesh as essence yields its place to a lyricism of Woman.

Why has this move been made, from symbol to lyric, "from awe to charm"? Barthes does not further explain why the cinema has given up its sense of the absolute in favor of its sense of the relative and the contingent. It may be that Valentino, Garbo, and Dietrich appeared as absolute difference, and inspired awe by doing so. Cinemagoers were not allowed to identify themselves with these divinities; they were supposed to give up for the time being their claims upon identity, sensing the limits they had come to and the abyss beyond. We are all historical now: existential, contingent, coming and going. Beauty, like truth and virtue and justice, is not absolute: no gods certify it, it gets by as best it can. Barthes thought that Audrey Hepburn represented the next phase after Garbo, the essence of beauty yielding to the lyric moments of beautiful existence, charm the best we can hope for and delight in:

> Viewed as a transition, the face of Garbo reconciles two iconographic ages, it assures the passage from awe to charm. As is well known, we are today at the other pole of this evolution: the face of Audrey Hepburn, for instance, is individualized, not only because of its peculiar thematics (woman as child, woman as kitten) but also because of her person, of an almost unique specification of the face, which has nothing of the essence left in it, but is constituted by an infinite complexity of morphological functions. As a language, Garbo's singularity was of the order of the concept, that of Audrey Hepburn is of the order of the substance. The face of Garbo is an Idea, that of Hepburn, an Event.[22]

It is still "seeing as." The specification of Hepburn's face points us toward kitten, child, or other constituents of a common world. If Garbo seems the Lady Beldonald of the silver screen, the reason is that both of them coincide with their appearance: nothing that would make for expression is allowed to obtrude. No wrinkle acknowledges the touch of life, time, or a master. The inferiority of Lady Beldonald to Garbo is evidenced by the fact that she needs her foils, Miss Dadd, Mrs. Brash, Miss What's-her-name. Garbo never needed a foil.

The democratization of beauty in Hollywood—and therefore in common desire—has gone much further in the years since Audrey Hepburn. No mystery inheres in the face of Julia Roberts. No secret is concealed in her eyes. Every attribute is endlessly available: fresh complexion, gleaming hair, teeth whiter-than-white, lavish mouth, indiscriminate smile, and a private life given over to visibility. We know nearly every detail of her life not because they have been pried loose from her intentions but because they are the terms in which she is presented to us: existential, historical, worldly. She is the felicity of bourgeois life, money and fame beyond the bourgeois norm merely indicating the extreme reach of gratification possible in that kind. Cinemagoers find her appearance charming because they have lost or given up any sense of essence or abstraction, of an unchanging idea behind the changing manifestations. They are not interested in the ecstasy of losing themselves in a face. They find it gratifying that Julia Roberts is so delightedly among her conditions, foils, and other instrumentalities: discarded lovers, Academy Awards, photographers, fans, the pleasure of being looked at. These are democratic pleasures, means by which a populace is kept diverted between one rhetorical occasion and the next.

4

The Force of Form

I

I have been postponing the consideration of beauty in relation
to form, apart from a few glancing references, because I find the
question difficult to articulate, much less answer. I am afraid that
it is the primary question, but it is also incorrigible. It has two
aspects. The hypostatic union of form and content, or form and
subject matter: how to say anything useful about it at this late
stage in its negotiation? The second aspect is even more difficult. It seems to me that form entails the conversion of matter,
so far as possible, to spirit. At the moment of conversion, form
and beauty seem to be one and the same. I don't see any difference between beauty and formal perfection: whatever can be said
about the one can be said with equal point about the other. Even
a landscape, which evidently is what it is when we see it, must
be looked at by someone as a certain genre of landscape before
it comes to its formal destiny. But the submission of matter to
spirit—or in Schiller's version, "beauty as freedom in its appearance"—can't be the whole story. Matter has its rights, too; it is
not always mere raw material. It is true that in our time matter,
in addition to the rights it deserves, has been given privileges
it doesn't deserve. It is only as a notion at the extreme longed-
for reach of possibility that matter could be given the decisive
privilege of pure materiality, uncontaminated by mind or desire.[1]
Some people want pure phenomena in which no act of mind is
involved. It follows that the same people want to dismiss spirit
as sheer mystification and send it slinking away as if it should

be ashamed of itself. For the moment I want to pose the question of beauty and form, so far as I can, in the context of modern poetry and criticism. I begin with two occasions.

The first occurred on December 8, 1936, when Wallace Stevens gave a lecture at Harvard University under the title "The Irrational Element in Poetry." His theme was the pressure of the contemporaneous on literature since the outbreak of the Great War. Before 1914, "the sea was full of yachts and the yachts were full of millionaires," or so it seemed. It was a time when "only maniacs had disturbing things to say."[2] But in December 1936 it appeared to Stevens and to other thoughtful people that "we look from an uncertain present toward a more uncertain future." As a result:

> One feels the desire to collect oneself against all this in poetry as well as in politics. If politics is nearer to each of us because of the pressure of the contemporaneous, poetry, in its way, is no less so and for the same reason. . . . The trouble is that the greater the pressure of the contemporaneous, the greater the resistance. Resistance is the opposite of escape. The poet who wishes to contemplate the good in the midst of confusion is like the mystic who wishes to contemplate God in the midst of evil. There can be no thought of escape. Both the poet and the mystic may establish themselves on herrings and apples. The painter may establish himself on a guitar, a copy of *Figaro* and a dish of melons. These are fortifyings, although irrational ones. The only possible resistance to the pressure of the contemporaneous is a matter of herrings and apples or, to be less definite, the contemporaneous itself. In poetry, to that extent, the subject is not the contemporane-

ous, because that is only the nominal subject, but the poetry of the contemporaneous. Resistance to the pressure of ominous and destructive circumstance consists of its conversion, so far as possible, into a different, an explicable, an amenable circumstance.[3]

The conversion entails, for the most part, "the transposition of an objective reality to a subjective reality." The transaction between reality and the sensibility of the poet, according to Stevens, is precisely that.[4] It may not be possible to change a brute fact to a more amenable fact—these are my words, not Stevens's—but the imagination can transform the appearances and the seemings, such that a subjective reality appears to emerge, at least while the going is good. The imagination, the "violence within," as Stevens elsewhere called it, engages with reality, the "violence without," and allows the poet to feel that a new reality, subjective in its main character, has been produced.[5] Many of Stevens's poems take this transformation as their motive. They begin with his conviction, expressed in "Notes toward a Supreme Fiction," that:

> From this the poem springs: that we live in a place
> That is not our own and, much more, not ourselves
> And hard it is in spite of blazoned days.[6]

Most of Stevens's poems are the work of unblazoned days in which the mind, as in Marvell's "The Garden," proposes to annihilate "all that's made to a green thought in a green shade." Or to a green image in a green shade, if we accept Levinas's insistence, in "Reality and Its Shadow," that "the most elementary procedure of art consists in substituting for the object its image":

> . . . its image, and not its concept. A concept is
> the object *grasped*, the intelligible object. Already

by action we maintain a living relationship with a real object; we grasp it, we conceive it. The image neutralizes this real relationship, this primary conceiving through action.[7]

Levinas trusted concepts more than images. He suspected that art was evasive and admired it only—as in Proust—when the artist detected his own evasiveness. But in a work of art there are no real objects—no bullfights in Hemingway, no bear hunts in Faulkner—there are only, as Susanne K. Langer says in *Feeling and Form*, virtual objects, images and shadows, offered to us in the hope of being perceived.[8] The motive of literature, according to Stevens, is to make the world appear to be our own, if not ourselves. We can live among those appearances. At least we are alert to them as possibilities of experience, and love them for that reason.

The second episode occurred in March 1938 when Archibald MacLeish published an essay called "Public Speech and Private Speech in Poetry." The gist of his argument was that modern poetry is characterized by a return to the "public speech" of the great ages of poetry; it involves a repudiation of the "private speech" characteristic of poetry in the periods of its decline.[9] MacLeish's chief exemplar of modern poetry was Yeats, "the best of modern poets," as he called him:

> Not in his capacity as a man of politics or as the director of a theatre but in his capacity as poet, Yeats has refused the customary costume. He is no self-conscious genius exploiting his difference from other men—and inventing differences where none exist. He is quite simply a man who is a poet. And his poetry is no escape from time and place and life and death but, on the contrary, the acceptance of these things and their embodiment.[10]

It is surprising that MacLeish adduced Yeats's "Byzantium" to illustrate "the strong presentness, the urgent voice" of public poetry. The poem is usually thought to be not at all a public poem: it seems to depend upon Yeats's individual if not eccentric notions of history and culture. There is still a lively dispute about the poem; whether it refers to the Byzantium of A.D. 500 or, as Empson argued, of A.D. 1000.[11] Most readers doubt that it has any public bearing. They don't even think its allusion to a particular place has much point. Byzantium is a symbolic region or state of being rather than a place. The poem does not float free of its context in Yeats's occult system though it is still ascertainable even if you haven't read *A Vision:* you can divine your way into it. We may pass over that consideration. MacLeish associated Yeats's later poems with Thomas Mann's assertion that in our time the destiny of man presents its meanings in political terms. MacLeish does not quote Mann but merely alludes to his view of modern reality and modern meanings, and apparently agrees with him[12] It is clear that MacLeish proposed to define the character of modern poetry by laudatory reference to the kind of poetry he himself wrote, rather than the different kinds written by Eliot and by Pound. The point of the essay was to give modern poetry a particularly grand status by associating it with Yeats, Mann, and the political definition of reality.

A few weeks later, someone brought MacLeish's essay to Yeats's attention. He was pleased to find himself celebrated for the "public" character of his poems. "That word which I had not thought of myself is a word I want," he told Dorothy Wellesley.[13] But he must have felt some misgiving about MacLeish's account of "Byzantium" and the later poems; he reported to Wellesley that MacLeish's essay "goes on to say that, owing to my age and my relation to Ireland, I was unable to use this 'public' language on what it evidently considered the right public material, politics."[14] Why should a poet give such privilege to politics? he may have asked himself. With the letter to Wellesley, Yeats enclosed a poem, "my reply," as he said: "It is not a real incident, but a moment of meditation."[15] The poem was "Politics." It uses as epigraph Mann's claim that in our time the destiny of man presents its meanings in political terms, but it seems to say that for politics one could just as cogently substitute sex or any other imperative value: religion, beauty, patriotism, justice, ambition, or another.

> How can I, that girl standing there,
> My attention fix
> On Roman or on Russian
> Or on Spanish politics?
> Yet here's a travelled man that knows
> What he talks about,
> And there's a politician
> That has read and thought,
> And maybe what they say is true
> Of war and war's alarms,
> But O that I were young again
> And held her in my arms![16]

The rhyming of "fix" and "politics" is Yeats's way of indicating that one may establish one's mind on many another value, equally compelling. The rhyming of "alarms" and "arms" has similar force, the monosyllable "arms" being as conclusive as its place at the end of the line and the end of the poem indicates. Yeats may have smarted at MacLeish's claim that he was too old and, because he was an Irishman, too isolated to bring his poetic genius to bear upon the real social, political, and economic issues of the time. His reply, this poem "Politics," claims that any major force of desire, any preoccupation—sexual desire, for instance—is capable of changing reality in its own favor: it has total ambition and for the time being at least the appearance of total capacity. Even in May 1938, with war's alarms irrefutable, reality was not entirely what Hitler, Roosevelt, and Chamberlain said it was. So Yeats's poem qualifies the claims of politics, war, and the materialities they mobilize by acknowledging the force of desire: none of these can be refuted. And the verse, after the rhetorical question at the beginning and the rough concession of the "here's" and "there's" and "maybe" of the second part, displaces one account of reality with the iambic certitude of another: "But O that I were young again / And held her in my arms!" The girl gets into the poem in the interpolated phrase—"that girl standing there"—even before the political question is announced. For the moment, objective reality has been displaced in favor of subjective reality. Or has appeared to be so displaced. "But O . . ." turns aside from official to unofficial reality. Desire and imagination have the same end in view. That end is the one that Hegel proposed in the preface to *Phenomenology of Spirit* when he claimed that one's sensory power is "so fast rooted in earthly things" that it requires force to raise it: "The Spirit shows itself as so impoverished that, like a wanderer in the desert craving a mere mouthful of water, it seems to crave for its refreshment only the bare feeling of the divine in general. By the little which now satisfies Spirit, we can measure the extent of its loss."[17] This does not authorize the conversion of matter to spirit, since spirit in Hegel is predicated on social rather than individual consciousness, but it offers a context of intersubjectivity in which particular acts of conversion, such as Stevens's and Yeats's, may be valued. Whether they are content with "only the bare feeling of the divine in general"—the divine having already been domesticated as the human imagination— would come up for consideration in particular readings of their poems. But even in such a limited form, these acts of conversion exert a certain pressure against the complacency of materialism and naturalism.

I have recited those two occasions to suggest that the beauty of literature seems to entail resistance to the official designations of reality. Even when it makes statements in ordinary language, a poem is not the sum of those statements. It maintains its autonomy—never absolute, however—by virtue of its form. Form is spirit as it makes its appearance and seems to realize its destiny. "As form," in Balthasar's version, "the beautiful can be materially grasped."[18] But materialism is not the theory of the grasping. Form is counter-statement, to use Kenneth Burke's term. Society makes statements and sends forth instructions, edicts, laws, definitions of reality. Literature makes counter-statements, Greek when the official designations are Roman. It makes these counter-statements not discursively but formally: as particular forms to be apprehended, achievements of invention and style, the right words in the right order, proprieties of cadence and invention. That is why it cannot be reduced to the journalism of themes or the commonplaces of social practice. Works of literature are forms of composition rather than forms of designation.[19]

II

In modern literature, construed under Eliot's authority rather than MacLeish's or even Yeats's, the main counter-statement is poetic form: not necessarily a special language or a particular diction or syntax but more often a common language with a distinctive turn of phrase and idiom. We do well to call this distinctiveness antinomian, as Pater does in *The Renaissance*, when we have in view a structure of values that stands aside from the official versions of reality and goes its own way, establishing itself on herrings and apples, if need be. If a work of literature challenges the official accounts of reality directly, we say that it is antithetical to them; but more often it is antinomian, it does not engage in conflict, it declares its presence and lets posterity come to a judgment. If it does not, it is kitsch. In *The Unbearable Lightness of Being* Kundera says that the May Day parade expresses not agreement with Communism but "an agreement with being as such."[20] That is what makes it kitsch. The early poetry of Eliot and Pound was antinomian, and it required a correspondingly disposed criticism, the New Criticism. The first generation of New Critics worked in response to a new literature that was as difficult then as it still is—"Hugh Selwyn Mauberley," "The Waste Land," *Ulysses, Charmes*—and they put their talents at the disposal of the new literature, the poetry of Eliot, Pound, Yeats, Rilke, Mallarmé, and Valéry, the fiction of Proust, Kafka, and Joyce. The early poems of Eliot and Pound preoccupied Leavis in *New Bearings in English Poetry*, Cleanth Brooks in *Modern Poetry and the Tradition*, Allen Tate in *On the Limits of Poetry*, and Blackmur in *The Expense of Greatness*. Those critics were more regularly antithetical than antinomian; they took as the common enemy the definitions of reality prescribed by science, positivism, naturalism, and the economics of power, especially the power of Wall Street and Washington. The notion of the literary work as a well-wrought urn was Brooks's way of asserting that such a work coincides with itself and that the coinciding is formal, an achievement of form. As form, it maintains its force—the force of a difficult unity—against the pressure of official considerations.

For similar reasons, the New Critics were much taken with Donne, Marvell, Herbert, and the Jacobean dramatists; not merely because Eliot instructed them in those mysteries but because the critics found in seventeenth-century poetry of a metaphysical bearing signal instances of the English language going about its independent business. John Crowe Ransom was slow to convert to the new poetry, and preferred meanwhile to talk in his own voice about Milton, with occasional meditations on Kant and Hegel. In England, Leavis, Richards, and Empson deemed Eliot to be crucial to their concerns, even when they wrote of issues other than his.

As a critic, Eliot was concerned with ways of writing, such that the resultant procedures would be impervious to the standard modes of discourse and would maintain themselves by minding their own strange business. A style, in that sense, would exert itself in local detail: the form of the poem would be the style at large, fully engaged with the issues and the possibilities it provoked. Styles worth attending to would correspond to the apprehension of the most subtle—the most subtly just—feelings in the case. Standard language is good enough if we are content with standard feelings. More complex feelings, those which are adequate to a more comprehensive sense of the issues at hand, require for expression—though expression cannot be separated from discovery and invention—the full resources of a language as capable as English or French. So Eliot was much taken with a passage of Tourneur's—or perhaps it is Middleton's—in *The Revenger's Tragedy*. In the third act, Vindice is meditating on the skull of his beloved:

> And now methinks I could e'en chide myself
> For doting on her beauty, though her death
> Shall be reveng'd after no common action.
> Does the silk-worm expend her yellow labours
> For thee? for thee does she undo herself?
> Are lordships sold to maintain ladyships
> For the poor benefit of a bewitching minute?
> Why does yon fellow falsify high-ways,
> And put his life between the judge's lips,
> To refine such a thing? keeps horse and men
> To beat their valours for her?[21]

In that passage—one of the most beautiful in Jacobean tragedy —Tourneur has discovered in the English language possibilities internal to itself; not by miming emotions deemed to be already there but by divining possibilities of language that precede their correlations in life; the silk-worm expending its "yellow labours," the repetition of "for thee" and its rhyme with "she," the ironic play on lordships and ladyships, "sold" furthering the note of "expend," and the "poor benefit of a bewitching minute." Eliot preferred an alternative reading, "bewildering minute," for which there is weak textual authority. The minute is poor by comparison with the gross expense of spirit in its service. In "To refine such a thing"—the verb lavishing itself on such a diminished object—"refine" gathers up the decadent implications from silk-worms and silks to ladyships and the sexuality of a bewitching minute. "Falsify high-ways" is difficult. I construe it as turning high-ways, which ought to be straight and true, into the low, crooked ways of falsehood and theft. The language seems to know not only what it means to say but what it feels about what it says: the movement of mind through the words is the adjudication of energy and its object. The linguistic effort is the effort of understanding not only what is there but how much its being there is worth in a large reckoning of the issues. Commenting on the passage in his essay on Massinger, Eliot notes "that perpetual slight alteration of language, words perpetually juxtaposed in new and sudden combinations, meanings perpetually *eingeschachtelt* into meanings, which evidences a very high development of the senses, a development of the English language which we have never perhaps equalled."[22] Quoting the same lines in "Tradition and the Individual Talent," he says:

> In this passage (as is evident if it is taken in its context) there is a combination of positive and negative emotions: an intensely strong attraction toward

beauty and an equally intense fascination by the ug-
liness which is contrasted with it and which destroys
it. This balance of contrasted emotion is in the dramatic situation to which the speech is pertinent, but
that situation alone is inadequate to it. This is, so
to speak, the structural emotion, provided by the
drama. But the whole effect, the dominant tone,
is due to the fact that a number of floating feelings, having an affinity to this emotion by no means
superficially evident, have combined with it to give
us a new art emotion.[23]

Presumably an "art emotion" is one that arises not from personal
circumstances but from expressive possibilities the artist has discovered in the particular practice of his medium. Tourneur discovered such an emotion in the act of writing, not prior to that in
an act of feeling. The development of the senses and the development of the English language minister alike to the production
of literary forms—sentences and phrases—that do not coincide
with the standard forms. "Yellow labours" is not standard English. The silk-worm expending her yellow labours for thee is a
discovery among the words. It is an antinomian invention, and
it makes a difficult form of beauty.

   If the standard available to poets in the years before and after
1914 had been adequate to their provocations, the poets would
have accepted them. Hardy, Graves, Frost, A. E. Housman,
Edward Thomas, and—for the most part—Yeats and Stevens
thought the common forms were adequate to begin with, and
they rang their sufficient changes on them in twists of idiom and
inflection. But the most exacting poets, notably Eliot, Pound,
and Hart Crane, were convinced that there was mainly discrepancy between their feelings and the forms at hand to express
them. Hence the critical concern with experimental forms and

the qualities in a poem or novel that keeps its counsel, refuses merely to transcribe its official subject. Ransom was again reluctant to change. He thought of poetic form on the analogy of the social ceremonies and decencies, as if writing a poem were an essay in courtship—which in some poems it is. In that respect the established forms were likely to be the right ones and the new ones were liable to be vulgar. "When a consensus of taste lays down the ordinance that the artist shall express himself formally, the purpose is evidently to deter him from expressing himself immediately."[24] Ransom thought that the established forms corresponded to codes of manners, all the better for being old and for counseling delay in their applications. The dispute between Ransom and Tate about "The Waste Land" arose from that consideration. Ransom maintained that the form of the poem was not justified by its apparent content. Tate thought it—in my view correctly—the only form of its extraordinarily complex feelings. Leavis, too, held that "The Waste Land" achieved the right form to intuit an "inclusive consciousness," adumbrated though not completed in the figure of Tiresias. No standard or inherited form could articulate such an intuition. Blackmur practiced a technical criticism of the detail of poems, the choice of words and the achieved organization among them, as in his early essays on Marianne Moore, Eliot, and Stevens, and he implied that the form of each achieved poem had the virtue of the distinctive diction and syntax he expounded. In the later essays of *The Lion and the Honeycomb* he wrote of behavior as the medium in which our lives take place, and of "theoretic form"—the phrase is Croce's—as the means by which we try to make sense of our behavior and bring it to the condition of executive form: that is, of performance.[25] So in poetry: the poem is always at a certain remove from the behavior or the feelings that incited it. Stevens's great labor, according to Blackmur, was to make the reality of what he merely felt pass into the impersonal reality of words, to reach the condition of form. Kenneth Burke approached the question of form as a rhetorical issue. He was a psychologist of literature and sometimes an anthropologist, chiefly interested in discovering in literature fundamental human structures and sequences — motives, as he called them. In the public house scene of "The Waste Land" at closing time we have the lines "Goonight Bill. Goonight Lou. Goonight May. Goonight. / Ta ta. Goonight. Goonight" followed by Ophelia's "Good night, ladies, good night, sweet ladies, good night, good night."[26] Why? No logic requires the progression. Burke says: "And suddenly the poet, feeling his release, drops into another good-night, a good-night with *désinvolture*, a good-night out of what was, within the conditions of the poem at least, a graceful and irrecoverable past."[27] The transition from the good-night of the public house to Ophelia's good-night is, Burke says, a "bold juxtaposition of one quality created by another, an association in ideas which, if not logical, is nevertheless emotionally natural."[28] It is emotionally natural, I assume, because we are genetically gifted with a sense of contrast and a sense of difference and more particularly with a sense of difference when it arises from a sense of the same. Burke addresses the issue because he regards form as rhetorical finesse, the arousing of a desire, followed in due but unexpected course by its satisfaction. This is formal perfection. If Burke could divine what is satisfying in the sequence I've quoted from "The Waste Land," he might be a little closer to understanding human motives, what makes the trajectory of our desires. We are gratified, it appears, by the unexpectedness of antinomian forms.

It is surprising, as Adorno remarks in *Aesthetic Theory,* how rarely theorists of aesthetics have reflected on the category of form. I am not discounting the work of theorists from Kant and Coleridge to Clive Bell, Kenneth Burke, Adrian Stokes, Henri Focillon, Jean Rousset, Leo Spitzer, and more recent critics, but the question of form has rarely been treated as the inescapable issue. This is strange, because form is the distinguishing characteristic of art; there is no reason to assume that it is unproblematically given, like the counting of syllables in an iambic pentameter. The obvious difficulty is that the question of form has been entangled in its relation to content. Louis Hjelmslev and Gérard Genette have proposed to get out of this entanglement by thinking of the opposite of form as substance rather than content, "the inert mass, either of extralinguistic reality (the substance of the content), or the means, phonic or otherwise, used by language (the substance of expression)."[29] The advantage of this change is that "formalism" will consist "not in privileging forms at the expense of meanings—which is senseless—but in considering meaning itself as a form imprinted in the continuity of the real." Language, as Genette says, "can 'express' the real only by articulating it, and this articulation is a system of signs, just as much on the level of the signified as on the level of the signifier."[30] If we try to separate form and substance, we turn form into an abstraction that habitually, Adorno says, "makes it an ally of reactionary art." But form can't be evaded; it is the coherence of the work of art—this is Adorno's main emphasis—"however self-antagonistic and refracted, through which every work of art separates itself from the merely existing." Form transfigures what otherwise merely exists, and by that transfiguration it maintains the validity of freedom. It is not creation from nothing, but a further creation from the otherwise created. Form is substance as imagined, not merely received: transfigured, not mimed. In the most authentic works of art, as Adorno has indicated, the authority that cultic objects exercised over their people has become the "immanent law of form."[31] These considerations seem to me much more convincing than the common arguments against Formalism: that it removes itself too quickly from the issues the poem deals with; that it conspires with the totalitarian zeal of the eye, the gaze; that in literary criticism it is so obsessed with the autonomy of the poem that it ignores the tendency of words to sprawl beyond their formal limits; and that a concern for beauty of form is an elitist satisfaction, morally disgusting while people are dying of hunger and disease. These arguments imply a claim for art that no serious critic makes. No one claims that a great symphony makes redundant the work of dentists, doctors, physicists, biologists, or politicians. Such a symphony makes the world a better place, richer in possibility and spirit; listening to it does not make people better or worse. But how we listen to it—as virtual time, as emerging form—has not been rendered a vain question by the Holocaust and AIDS. Aesthetics is in no danger of being demystified by irony or critique. I agree with Simon Jarvis's attack on "the widespread assumption that the difficulties associated with such aporetic categories as nature, subjectivity, beauty, goodness and truth can be overcome simply by suppressing, avoiding, or junking those categories—or by subjecting them to 'ideology-critique,' that is to say, to ideology."[32] But beauty is saved from that distress only by its articulation as particular forms.

I find it strange, therefore, that some teachers of literature are encouraging their students to disregard the radical question of form and the values it entails and to concern themselves instead—diagnostic intent being the sole mode of attention—with the extractable ideological stance of the work in hand. They are prepared to settle for commonplace attitudes and notions rather than rise to the occasion of the most complex structures of feeling. The particular qualities that justify the writing and reading of literature are precisely those which such teachers are encouraging their students to ignore, in the interests, apparently, of a seminar that may be thought of as lively. They are willing to set aside the difficult virtues of irony and skepticism for the trivial satisfaction of feeling morally superior to whatever they read. In irony, as in the antinomian gesture, one turns aside from the prevailing commonplaces of discourse. Skepticism is the habit of doing so, though it is a habit we are sometimes impelled to break. In colleges and universities we are regularly admonished to attend to our students' interests and to assume that these are popular, contemporary and discursive. "Content analysis" is supposedly enough. I can't imagine that such advice would be proffered, and with such reiterative emphasis, to teachers of mathematics, physics, or a foreign language.

III

Not that form is easy. Marshall Brown has remarked, thinking it a problem, that we don't know what form is. But we know, as he does, that a work of literature, so far as it is formally achieved, "holds form in reserve as its power to direct the chaotic forces within it." Form is the achieved, purposed deployment of energy, energy available on need and not there till looked for: it is never found before the need of it. As Brown says, "Form retains its value only so long as it cannot be grasped or reduced to theme or idea."[33] That is why it may be sensed in advance but can't be known: it is why, too, the plot of a novel is grasped as the force of organization that comes after the form, as if proving that the form was there, but only *in potentia*, all along.

It is disturbing that critics whom one would suppose to have a care for the distinguishing powers of a work of art are willing to deride the consideration of form. Derrida, as a case in point, has spoken of form in an invidious relation to force. In an early essay on Jean Rousset, he claimed that "form fascinates when one no longer has the force to understand force from within itself: that is, to create." In the heliocentric metaphysic, as Derrida called it, which is founded on metaphors of light and dark—truth as light, error as dark—force has ceded its place to

eidos, "that is, to the form that is visible to the metaphoric eye."
Force "has already been separated from its sense of force, as the
quality of music is separated from itself in acoustics." Derrida
does not simply juxtapose force and form, recognizing both as
if they were on the same level of being; he seeks "new concepts
and new models," an economy that "escapes such oppositions."
It is as if he resented the destiny by which force takes any form,
especially the one by which it comes into its own. He wants to
"produce a force of dislocation that spreads itself throughout
the entire system."[34] Why should he want such a force, except
that he thinks of form as necessarily static and spatial; as if it
sought the stability of presence he deplored in the Structuralisms
of Lévi-Strauss and Saussure? Perhaps he is thinking of form
as beauty, and of force as a better value, the sublime, but even
if he is, there is no merit in positing an invidious distinction.
The reason why Joseph Frank's concept of "spatial form" is misleading, in its presumed bearing upon certain works of modern
literature — *Nightwood, Ulysses* — is that these works, too, have to
be read temporally, one word after another. In those books, the
achievement of form acknowledges time. Dominant images in a
play of Shakespeare's may appear to have a quasi-spatial character, but they haven't; they establish points of thematic pressure
without retarding the dynamic movement of the play. The concept of the "open work" that Luigi Pareyson and Umberto Eco
have described might appear to refute every theory of form. Such
work — Stockhausen's *Klavierstücke XI*, for instance — seems to
give each interpreter the freedom of completing the work. But it
still requires the interpreter to interpret; and each performance
of the work is just as closed as the reading of a traditional novel.
Even if the work is a "work in progress" or what Eco calls a
"work in movement," each performance of it puts a stop to the
movement.[35] Mobiles such as Calder's — another of Eco's instances of open work — may be "elementary structures which can

move in the air and assume different spatial dispositions: they continuously create their own space and the shapes to fill it,"[36] but on every occasion on which I look at a mobile, I bring its mobility to an end, while my attention lasts. The experience is a speeded-up version of walking around any free-standing sculpture: you can see it from only one perspective at a time. Derrida is responsive to the rush or the blow of force, but only so long as it remains independent of its discovered or invented form. When I look at a wave breaking along a beach, I see a force becoming its form. Derrida has no sense of form as force proceeding to its discovered end, as in music, dance, and drama. He thinks of it only in picturesque or architectural terms, and resents its semblance of stability.

Leavis, too, is another case in point. He found the form of Eliot's early poems convincing and admired in them "the extreme discipline of continence in respect of affirmation." But he rebuked Eliot, many years later, for the passage in "Burnt Norton" about the Chinese jar:

> Words move, music moves
> Only in time; but that which is only living
> Can only die. Words, after speech, reach
> Into the silence. Only by the form, the pattern,
> Can words or music reach
> The stillness, as a Chinese jar still
> Moves perpetually in its stillness.[37]

Those lines seemed to Leavis a scandal because they offered, he thought, a value upon which conviction might rest. The complaint is not justified. What Eliot calls "the silence" isn't a state of being to rest on but a state, otherwise nameless, to aspire to. "The form, the pattern" isn't something known in advance: if it were, one of those nouns would be enough. The Chinese jar still moving perpetually in its stillness doesn't designate a spiritual end in the sense of a conclusion that coincides with itself. The whole passage in "Burnt Norton" has to do with time, and the possibility of redeeming time: it is really about prayer, the value of which entails its not resting on satisfactions or complacencies. Like prayer, it hopes to partake of the distinction between mere chronological time—one damn thing after another—and time redeemed in value and sense. Theologians speak of the distinction as one between *tempus* and *aevum*. Leavis's complaint presupposes that what he calls "a certain restriction in the nourishing interests"—such as he ascribes to the later Eliot—is the cause of one's believing anything. But he doesn't hold it against Lawrence that he believed so much. Agnostics believe as much as Christians—they just believe different things, a point Eliot made in showing that Bertrand Russell believed as much as Augustine did. On the passage in "Burnt Norton," Leavis evidently thought that Eliot was claiming to know, as a poet, what in fact he prayed to believe as a Christian, a penitent, a soul in torment.[38]

The emphasis we need, if we are to avoid setting up yet another opposition between force and form, is to apprehend form in the idiom of time and sequence. In *The Sense of an Ending* Frank Kermode speaks up for "submission to the fictive patterns," but he doesn't think of patterns as picturesque or spatial:

> For one thing, a systematic submission of this kind is almost another way of describing what we call "form." "An inter-connexion of parts all mutually implied"; a duration (rather than a space) organizing the moment in terms of the end, giving meaning to the interval between tick and tock because we humanly do not want it to be an indeterminate interval between the tick of birth and the tock of death. That is a way of speaking in temporal terms of literary form.[39]

The critic who set aside the consideration of poetic form most assertively is Paul de Man. He was a remarkably close reader, but he did not read in the interests of a poem or a novel. Or in the interests of his own pleasure. He was a grim reader, hostile as if on principle to any sign of inventiveness, wit, the gypsy phrase, or memorable cadence. Literature and philosophy were alike in being places of figuration, and he wrote of them in the same determined spirit. He paid little or no attention to the considerations that make a poem what it is, not merely an instance of Poetry but that particular poem. At one point he acknowledged that literature is "the only form of language free from the fallacy of unmediated expression," but he did not indicate where that freedom was to be found and enjoyed. Where else could it be found but in form? But de Man dealt with the question of poetic forms only by brushing it aside.[40]

The essay on Rilke is a case in point. De Man is concerned with "Rilke's text," as he calls it, but only incidentally and opportunistically with his texts, the individual poems. We normally associate this practice with Poulet and other phenomenological critics. De Man's essay on Rilke shows him moving between phenomenology and Structuralism. The question he proposes is "whether Rilke's text turns back upon itself in a manner that puts the authority of its own affirmations in doubt, especially when these affirmations refer to the modes of writing that it advocates." The text is evidently Rilke's complete works, considered as if they amounted to a single poem with qualities from which de Man selects one to support a thesis. He maintains that "the determining figure of Rilke's poetry is that of chiasmus, the crossing that reverses the attributes of words and of things." Of the poems in Rilke's *New Poems*, de Man says:

When they describe personages or settings, they have often been so caught in a stylized perception that they have become like icons, emblems of a feeling or of a destiny as sharply circumscribed as are the properties of things. It soon appears that all these objects share a similar fundamental structure: they are conceived in such a way as to allow a reversal of their categorical properties, and this reversal enables the reader to conceive of properties that would normally be incompatible (such as inside/outside, before/after, death/life, fiction/reality, silence/sound) as complementary. . . . If we question why such or such an object inscribed in the *New Poems* has compellingly attracted Rilke's attention (or why he deliberately selected it), the answer will always be that it forced itself upon him because its attributes allow for such a reversal and for such an (apparent) totalization.

The conclusion to be drawn, according to de Man, is that Rilke's "notion of figural language eliminates all truth-claims from his discourse."[41]

In view of the interests disclosed in these sentences, it is not surprising that de Man regarded literary forms as mere local seductions. He was concerned not with poems as achieved compositions but with language as a system of rhetorical figures. But the animus he displayed against any critical concern with the form of a poem still calls for comment. I think he denounced an interest in form because he hoped to deprive art of its creative privilege. In an early essay he claimed, with evident pleasure, that formalist criticism was a dead end. I'll rehearse the essay to see what it entails.

De Man was concerned with Richards's *Principles of Liter-*

ary Criticism and, more particularly, with Empson's *Seven Types of Ambiguity* and *Some Versions of Pastoral*. He concentrated on Empson's account, in the book on ambiguity, of the fourth line of Shakespeare's sonnet 73:

> That time of year thou mayst in me behold
> When yellow leaves, or none, or few, do hang
> Upon those boughs which shake against the cold,
> Bare, ruined choirs, where late the sweet birds sang.

Empson says that the comparison between the complaining speaker and the bare, ruined choirs

> holds for many reasons; because ruined monastery choirs are places in which to sing, because they involve sitting in a row, because they are made of wood, are carved into knots and so forth, because they used to be surrounded by a sheltering building crystallised out of the likeness of a forest, and coloured with stained glass and painting like flowers and leaves, because they are now abandoned by all but the grey walls coloured like the skies of winter, because the cold and Narcissistic charm suggested by choir-boys suits well with Shakespeare's feeling for the object of the Sonnets, and for various sociological and historical reasons (the protestant destruction of monasteries; fear of puritanism), which it would be hard now to trace out in their proportions.

These reasons, and many more relating the simile to its place in the sonnet, Empson says, "must all combine to give the line its beauty, and there is a sort of ambiguity in not knowing which of them to hold most clearly in mind." This is involved, he says, "in all such richness and heightening of effect, and the machinations of ambiguity are among the very roots of poetry." [42] De Man doesn't dispute the semantic stretch of this analysis, but he elucidates the metaphor differently:

> . . . instead of setting up an adequation between two experiences, and thereby fixing the mind on the repose of an established equation, it deploys the initial experience into an infinity of associated experiences that spring from it. In the manner of a vibration spreading in infinitude from its center, metaphor is endowed with the capacity to situate the experience at the heart of a universe that it generates. It provides the ground rather than the frame, a limitless anteriority that permits the limiting of a specific entity. Experience sheds its uniqueness and leads instead to a dizziness of the mind. Far from referring back to an object that would be its cause, the poetic sign sets in motion an imaging activity that refers to no object in particular. The "meaning" of the metaphor is that it does not "mean" in any definite manner. [43]

But the relation between the declining speaker, the waning year, and the branches of the trees doesn't imply an adequation between the experiences or the repose of the mind on an established equation. As in the best metaphors, you have to sense the awkwardness the feeling has had to ride across to achieve this particular representation. In a metaphysical conceit, you are alert to the considerations that threaten to make the figure absurd before coming to the better sense that it's not, after all, absurd: only your squeamishness was a nuisance. Where Empson claimed that "a word or a grammatical structure is effective in several ways at once," and that it is up to the reader to decide which of the relations to hold most clearly in mind, de Man claimed that "a fundamental ambiguity is constitutive of all poetry," and that it proceeds "from the deep division of Being itself." "The ambiguity poetry speaks of is the fundamental one that prevails between the world of the spirit and the world of sentient substance: to ground itself, the spirit must turn itself into sentient substance, but the latter is knowable only in its dissolution into non-being. The spirit cannot coincide with its object and this separation is infinitely sorrowful."[44] De Man speaks further—he goes far to seek disquietude—of the "contradictory relations between natural being and the being of consciousness," but he doesn't say who utters the contradiction or who feels it as contradiction or catastrophe. He cites Empson's seventh type of ambiguity as evidence, but that type is no evidence at all; it has nothing to say about alleged contradictory relations between natural being and the being of consciousness. The ambiguity of that type occurs, according to Empson, "when the two meanings of the word, the two values of the ambiguity, are the two opposite meanings defined by the context, so that the total effect is to show a fundamental division in the writer's mind." A division in a writer's mind proves only that his feelings are complex and discrepant, not that language is a dud. Empson's prize example is "Buckle!" in Hopkins's "The Windhover." Empson thinks it can mean "collapse like a bicycle wheel" or "buckle like a military belt for heroic action." But if he ascribes this contradiction to a fundamental division in the writer's mind, then a sense of this division is part of the reader's experience in reading the poem: no dizziness is entailed. Nothing requires us to posit, with de Man, contradictory relations between natural being and the being of consciousness, unless for other reasons we want to do so. Even if we agree with his metaphysics of doom, there is still no reason to think that a formalist criticism is useless. Such a criticism is useful precisely because it respects the sense in which the formal destiny of a poem resists assimilation to any of the standard patterns of assurance.

De Man concludes his essay by claiming that "after the writings of an Empson, little is left of the scientific claims of formalist criticism."[45] I don't know which formalist critic de Man has in mind. I've never heard of such a claim. The New Critics whom de Man describes as formalist wouldn't have thought their criticism strengthened by having the support of science. Like Pound, Empson admired the way scientists went about their business, but he didn't think a poem was the better for being approved by the physics master. He thought that interpreting a poem was like going to a play of Shakespeare's at the Globe: there was something in it for everybody, from groundlings to scholars. If some readers of Sonnet 73 think of the destruction of the monasteries—as I do—when they come to the bare, ruined choirs, there is no merit in pulling a long face about it and telling them to stick to a more ascertainable point. The sonnet is not reducible to the destruction of the monasteries, but I see no harm and some good in allowing the historical reference to come into the periphery of the reading: it extends the spread of the poem, brings in more aspects.

But the main problem with de Man's essay is that he has not shown any relation between the inherent ambiguity of poetry and the allegedly dead-end quality of formalist criticism. Nothing in Empson's commentary on "The Windhover" rules out a formalist analysis of that poem. Evidently de Man has an interest in showing a relation between ambiguity and the alleged categorical failure of formalist criticism, because he thinks of form as the most reassuring factor in reading a poem, as in writing one, and he wants to remove the felicity of it. Surely he cannot be thinking of form as providing the security of discovering that a Shakespearean sonnet has indeed fourteen lines linked by rhymes and other technical features? De Man has no good reason for thinking that form, as the principle of energy that directs a poem from first word to last, puts a stop to the chaos it engaged, or that the sea is calm in the end that was choppy at the start. "The surface of the blackened river" continues to be "a face that sweats with tears."[46] Only one's sense of that continuance, and of the rush and swell beneath the river, has changed. Form is inspiriting because of the possible order it divines, but it is not money in the bank.

V

The main reason why we should not make any concession in disputes on form is that form is the consideration, the value, on which the relative autonomy of artistic work has depended since about 1835. Recognition of artistic form, and of the values its achievement carries, is the ground upon which writers, readers, critics, and intellectuals are constituted. Pierre Bourdieu is our best guide to these matters, so much so that I shall have virtually nothing to add to his arguments in *Distinction; Language and Symbolic Power;* and *The Rules of Art,* especially this last. I shall merely bring together a number of themes which in Bourdieu's books are often separated by other issues. In *The Rules of Art,* with Flaubert mainly in mind, Bourdieu says that "a power must be affirmed that belongs to art to constitute everything aesthetically by virtue of form."[47] Form is the value which enables writers—Bourdieu names Flaubert, Taine, and Renan—to stand aside from political issues, even in the midst of public clamor, and to mind their own artistic business. It is also the value that permits writers to take part in political conflict, but with weapons "that are not those of politics."[48] Zola's intervention in the Dreyfus Affair was animated by precisely the same values that impelled him to defend Manet's paintings. The very existence of an avant-garde presupposes the values embodied in a work of art by virtue of its form. When writers insist on their independence from social, religious, and political forces, it is by appeal, silently or not, to the form of their writings: they inherit the victories of Manet against the Académie, and of Flaubert against the novel of commerce. More specifically: it is by appeal to the unquestionable character of artistic form that the aesthetic mode of perception "situates the principle of 'creation' within the representation and not within the thing represented," an act never so fully asserted "as when it is able to constitute aesthetically the base or vulgar objects of the modern world."[49] If artists have been able to establish what J. C. Sloane called "the neutrality of the subject,"[50] it is because they have shown that creative force is not a force alternative to form but itself the particular form of its erupting into being.

VI

I don't think it is necessary to rehearse the various attempts that have been made to distinguish one kind of form from another; such as Coleridge's distinction between organic form, the work of nature as in Yeats's great-rooted chestnut-tree, and mechanic form, the work of will by which we stamp our authority on an apparently plastic and passive substance. I leave aside, too, the differences among forms as they have been observed by Focillon, Panofsky, Langer, Stokes, Kenneth Burke, Richard Klein, and other writers. But I should end with an example of form as—in Burke's terms—the creation of a desire, and the adequate satisfaction of that desire. This satisfaction, as Burke says, at times may involve a temporary set of frustrations, "but in the end these frustrations prove to be simply a more involved kind of satisfaction, and furthermore serve to make the satisfaction of fulfillment more intense."[51]

In the first chapter of *The Great Gatsby* Fitzgerald's narrator Nick Carraway concedes that "there was something gorgeous" about Gatsby, "some heightened sensitivity to the promises of life," "an extraordinary gift for hope."[52] The first part of the novel is emphatic in such sentiments, the diction featuring such words as these: summer, hope, responsiveness, riotous, glowing, romantic, smiles, mystery, beauty, wonder, illusion, voice, and "blue gardens." The second part is much more limited in its diction: it is dominated by the ashheaps, the heat and noise of the room in the Plaza Hotel, George Wilson's garage. Typical words are these: careless, incoherent. This part of the novel is given over to images of deception, charlatanry, violence, trivial lives, the crash of broken promises. But the romance of hope, its freshness day by day, has been given to us as a motif: a desire has been incited. The law of form prescribes that the desire be eventually satisfied. By the last chapter, Gatsby, Myrtle, and Wilson are dead, Tom and Daisy are together in their vast carelessness, and Nick is going back to the Midwest. The desire set astir by talk of hope and promise in the early chapters has been impeded through many frustrating pages, but it has not been suppressed. I quote the last page of the novel, where Nick is on the beach, looking at the houses on Long Island Sound:

> Most of the big shore places were closed now and there were hardly any lights except the shadowy, moving glow of a ferryboat across the Sound. And as the moon rose higher the inessential houses began to melt away until gradually I became aware of the old island here that flowered once for Dutch sailors' eyes—a fresh, green breast of the new world. Its vanished trees, the trees that had made way for Gatsby's house, had once pandered in whispers to the last and greatest of all human dreams; for a tran-

sitory enchanted moment man must have held his breath in the presence of this continent, compelled into an aesthetic contemplation he neither understood nor desired, face to face for the last time in history with something commensurate to his capacity for wonder.

And as I sat there brooding on the old, unknown world, I thought of Gatsby's wonder when he first picked out the green light at the end of Daisy's dock. He had come a long way to this blue lawn, and his dream must have seemed so close that he could hardly fail to grasp it. He did not know that it was already behind him, somewhere back in that vast obscurity beyond the city, where the dark fields of the republic rolled on under the night.

Gatsby believed in the green light, the orgastic future that year by year recedes before us. It eluded us then, but that's no matter — tomorrow we will run faster, stretch out our arms farther . . . And one fine morning—

So we beat on, boats against the current, borne back ceaselessly into the past.[53]

There is a problem with this passage. Nothing we have been shown of Nick Carraway makes it likely that he would be able to think those thoughts or entertain those visions. Not for the first time, Fitzgerald steps forward and takes over the narrative. He does Nick's thinking for him. It is rhetorically crucial that the desire for hope and expansiveness be appeased. Whether we take the sentences as Nick's or Fitzgerald's, they are alluding to things neither of them could directly know. The mode of thinking is "the romantic," as Henry James called it in the preface to *The American*. The romantic stands, James says, "for the things that, with all the facilities in the world, all the wealth and all the courage and all the wit and all the adventure, we never can directly know; the things that can reach us only through the beautiful circuit and subterfuge of our thought and our desire."[54] In *The Great Gatsby* it is our desire more than our thought. Nothing in the book up to this page has suggested that it would end on this note: it might have ended merely with muddle. The last page, which is the third part of the novel however brief, is antinomian to the crabbed realism of the plot, Tom's intrigue to have Gatsby blamed for Myrtle's death and murdered by Wilson. The last page is an instance of what Burke calls "qualitative progression," the movement from one motif to the next effected not by narrative logic but by likeness or difference, as in the "Goodnight" scene of "The Waste Land." If we stretch a point and attribute the passage to Nick, we can say that with the rising moon, he must see the houses as inessential: they must melt away before he can enjoy the subterfuge of his romantic vision, Long Island as it seemed to the eyes of the first Dutch sailors. He must go back to the beginning, identifying it with the essence of the experience, so that when it comes into temporal existence it may thrive. "Flowered" is the first word of his desire, and the motif is developed in "breast" and "new" and "enchanted." It comes to its first satisfaction in "wonder." But the vision acknowledges discrepancy: the trees pandering in whispers, the enchanted moment itself passing. The word "wonder" is then recovered from its abstraction, "man," and given to Gatsby. The light at the end of Daisy's dock is called green because that is what it was and Gatsby believes in it as the light of the orgastic future, but his lawn is blue because blue is the color held in reserve for the imagination, as in Stevens's "The Man with the Blue Guitar." So to Gatsby's dream, mortified by another discrepancy since it "was already behind him"—though he didn't know it—in Louisville and among the dark fields of the republic. The last sentence may be compared for eloquence with the second of Hart Crane's "Voyages":

> Bind us in time, O Seasons clear, and awe.
> O minstrel galleons of Carib fire,
> Bequeath us to no earthly shore until
> Is answered in the vortex of our grave
> The seal's wide spindrift gaze toward paradise.

In the end, Nick gives up the privilege of his sole self and takes on the experience of an entire people, the communal "we." It is an astounding act of identification. "So we beat on, boats against the current, borne back ceaselessly into the past." After "And one fine morning," we expected a vision of the future. Instead, we get the enchanted past. But what we are given turns out to be, however unexpectedly, what we desired. In this episode the law of form is based if not on a metaphysics of Natural Law then on a metabiology, a common vernacular of bodies, their rhythms as appeasing as the circulation of the blood. The interpolated phrase "boats against the current" is a musical variation on the theme of the sentence, linked to it by the alliteration of "beat" and "boats" and "borne." The desire for romance, beauty, wonder, and a transfigured world is satisfied in the steady monosyllables, "So we beat on."

5

Ruskin, Venice, and the
Fate of Beauty

I

The idea of the equal and simultaneous fellowship of truth, virtue, and beauty, "the complete consort dancing together," belongs to the realm of hope: it cannot be pointed to in common practice, unless Balthasar's practice becomes common. For the time being we have to settle for a worldly correlative of it, as in Ruskin. I think of him in three emphases. One: Ruskin, even more thoroughly than Morris, practiced the sense of beauty as a civic value. Two: Ruskin's engagement with Turner's paintings exemplifies a nearly ideal form of paying attention to beauty. And three: Ruskin's long and often angry relation to Venice shows us what it means to care for cultural and political practices under the auspices of beauty.

In the fourth section—the Postscript—of the preface to his translation of *The Bible of Amiens*, Proust brings forward a consideration of Ruskin that, if true, would reduce our appreciation of his work. He quotes from *The Stones of Venice* the last page of the chapter on St. Mark's, the passage that comes immediately after Ruskin's assertion that the shrine of St. Mark's, in the hearts of the old Venetian people, was far more than a place of worship: "It was at once a type of the Redeemed Church of God, and a scroll for the written word of God."[1] The page quoted brings the chapter to a punitive end:

Not in the wantonness of wealth, not in vain ministry to the desire of the eyes or the pride of life, were those marbles hewn into transparent strength, and those arches arrayed in the colours of the iris. There is a message written in the dyes of them, that once was written in blood; and a sound in the echoes of their vaults, that one day shall fill the vault of heaven, — "He shall return to do judgment and justice." The strength of Venice was given her, so long as she remembered this: her destruction found her when she had forgotten this; and it found her irrevocably, because she forgot it without excuse. Never had city a more glorious Bible. Among the nations of the North, a rude and shadowy sculpture filled their temples with confused and hardly legible imagery; but, for her, the skill and the treasures of the East had gilded every letter, and illumined every page, till the Book-Temple shone from afar off like the star of the Magi. In other cities, the meetings of the people were often in places withdrawn from religious association, subject to violence and to change; and on the grass of the dangerous rampart, and in the dust of the troubled street, there were deeds done and counsels taken, which, if we cannot justify, we may sometimes forgive. But the sins of Venice, whether in her palace or in her piazza, were done with the Bible at her right hand. The walls on which its testimony was written were separated but by a few inches of marble from those which guarded the secrets of her councils, or confined the victims of her policy. And when in her last hours she threw off all shame and all restraint, and the great square of the city became filled with the madness of the

whole earth, be it remembered how much her sin
was greater, because it was done in the face of the
House of God, burning with the letters of His Law.
Mountebank and masquer laughed their laugh, and
went their way; and a silence has followed them,
not unforetold; for amidst them all, through century after century of gathering vanity and festering
guilt, that white dome of St. Mark's had uttered
in the dead ear of Venice, "Know thou, that for all
these things God will bring thee into judgment."
(*CW* 10: 141–142)

Proust quotes that passage to support his charge that falsehood,
in whatever magnificent and tempting forms, had crept into
Ruskin's intellectual sincerity and taken up residence there. He
was guilty of idolatry, the sin that Ruskin himself described in
Lectures on Art, "the serving with the best of our hearts and
minds some dear and sad fantasy which we have made for ourselves, while we disobey the present call of the Master, who is
not dead, and who is not fainting under His cross, but requiring
us to take up ours" (*CW* 20: 66). Proust claims to find in Ruskin
"sincerity struggling against idolatry"—"ce besoin de sincérité
qui lutte contre l'idolâtrie, qui proclame sa vanité, qui humilie
la beauté devant le devoir, fût-il inesthétique."[2] The particular
form the struggle took was a confounding of aesthetic and moral
values. Ruskin was not like Racine, Tolstoy, and Maeterlinck,
"aesthetic at first and moral afterwards." In Ruskin, "morality
claims its rights within the very heart of aesthetics," but perhaps never frees itself from aesthetics as completely as it did in
Racine, Tolstoy, and Maeterlinck:[3]

The doctrines [that Ruskin] professed were moral
doctrines and not aesthetic doctrines, and yet he
chose them for their beauty. And since he did not

wish to present them as beautiful but as true, he was forced to deceive himself about the nature of the reasons that made him adopt them. Hence there was such a continual compromising of conscience, that immoral doctrines sincerely professed would perhaps have been less dangerous to the integrity of his mind than those moral doctrines in which affirmation is not absolutely sincere, as they are dictated by an unavowed aesthetic preference.[4]

The passage from *The Stones of Venice* seemed to Proust a case in point: he found it beautiful but thought that it was based on something false. In theory, the beauty it appealed to was subordinated to moral sentiment and truth, but in fact, moral sentiment and truth were subordinated to aesthetic sentiment, and to aesthetic sentiment warped, Proust maintained, by endless compromises:

> Had Ruskin been entirely sincere with himself, he would not have thought that the crimes of the Venetians had been more inexcusable and more severely punished than those of other men because they possessed a church in multicolored marble instead of a cathedral in limestone, because the palace of the Doges was near St. Mark's instead of at the other end of the city, and because in Byzantine churches the biblical text, instead of being simply represented as in the sculpture of the churches of the North, is accompanied, in the mosaics, by letters that form a quotation from the Gospel or the prophecies.[5]

Proust also thought it evidence of idolatry that "the beauty of Ruskin's images was intensified and corrupted by the pride of referring to the sacred text."[6]

These are formidable considerations. Beyond calling it idolatry, Proust does not specify the falsehood that allegedly corrupted Ruskin's values. I would give it two names: Byron and Carlyle. Ruskin received from Byron, more resoundingly than from Wordsworth, Shelley, or any other English or French source, the motif of Venetian decay. Byron's "Ode to Venice" and the fourth Canto of *Childe Harold's Pilgrimage* presented the fall of Venice as that of one great city among many, the fall of Rome being in that Canto the most dreadful. More than any other poet, Byron, as he wrote of himself, "bodied forth the heated mind, / Forms from the floating wreck which Ruin leaves behind."[7] He lavished on Venice, brought low by Austria in 1815, the largesse of pathos and plangency that Ruskin thought to extend. But Ruskin denounced where Byron mourned. He excoriated the Venice that Byron took as an instance of inevitable decay. Carlyle damaged Ruskin by making him think that the style of *On Heroes* (1841) and *Past and Present* (1843), familiar as it was with the glamour of Byron's poetry, should be emulated as a style good for every occasion of praise or blame.

But Proust was wrong to rebuke Ruskin for quoting the Bible, the book that, more than any other, took possession of his mind from earliest childhood. Besides, Ruskin's allusions to Genesis and Ecclesiastes in the passage from *The Stones of Venice* are not there primarily to enhance the majesty of his denunciation but to give it a particular setting. The theme of the passage is not, in a merely general sense, the Venetian obscenity of conducting sinister politics among holy images. It is more specific. Ruskin is invoking the episode in Mark in which Christ "cast out them that sold and bought in the temple, and overthrew the tables of the moneychangers, and the seats of them that sold doves." "And he taught, saying unto them, Is it not written, 'My house shall be called of all nations the house of prayer'? but ye have made it a den of thieves" (Mark 11: 15, 17). Ruskin is claiming

Christ's authority for expelling the thieves, however belatedly and in words rather than deeds, from the shrine he declared a type of the Redeemed Church of God and a scroll for the written word of God. The crimes of Venice were indeed greater—more disgusting—than they would otherwise be judged to have been, because of the vulgarity of ignoring the holy images that surrounded them.

II

Proust accuses Ruskin of a defect of character, but what I find in this episode are two rival senses of beauty. Proust's sense of beauty is a feeling for the sacred quality of occasions and remembrances: his response to these provocations is given in continuities and nuanced alterations of sensibility. Ruskin's sense of beauty saw it as an intrication of forms, reaching a state of rest in the end but only after conflicts of principle, good and evil, roses and cankerworms. Two traditions are in question. I can give a bare notion of Ruskin's by referring to two considerations. The first is brought forward in Northrop Frye's *Anatomy of Criticism*, where the issue is between Ruskin and Arnold. Arnold has deplored a passage from Ruskin's *Munera Pulveris*, thinking it provincial. But Frye takes Ruskin's side:

> Here it is Arnold who is the provincial. Ruskin has learned his trade from the great iconological tradition which comes down through Classical and Biblical scholarship into Dante and Spenser, both of whom he had studied carefully, and which is incorporated in the medieval cathedrals he had pored over in such detail. Arnold is assuming, as a universal law of nature, certain "plain sense" critical axioms which were hardly heard of before Dryden's

time and which can assuredly not survive the age of
Freud and Jung and Frazer and Cassirer.[8]

Frye would perhaps concede that the Arnoldian style of criticism—let us say from Arnold to Eliot and Frye himself—has
established itself for urbane and intelligent readers on occasions
of civil discourse. He might even agree that Byron and Carlyle damaged Ruskin's common style. But he would insist that
the Arnoldian style is only one option among several: it is not
mandatory. Ruskin's style, and the sense of beauty that animated it, came from a different tradition, Hebraic rather than
Greek. He had just as much authority as Arnold had, the authority of Gothic generosity and verve.

The second reference I need goes along with Frye's argument.
In *Darwin's Plots* Gillian Beer quotes Ruskin's allusion in *Love's
Meinie* to the "filthy heraldries which record the relation of
humanity to the ascidian and the crocodile," and she argues that
the sentence, which cannot be called urbane, is culturally explicable. The loss of teleological order was countered in Victorian
prose by the authority of the speaking voice. Ruskin's reference
to filthy heraldries has only the authority of his voice, and for
readers hospitable to his tradition it is enough. Beer also notes
how the authority of voice enabled the "rapid transformation
of one kind of reference into another—economics into art history into race theory."[9] The mobility of the speaking voice made
it easy to go from one discipline to another without worrying
about the demarcation of each. Carlyle complained to Emerson—without thinking that he himself might bear some responsibility—that Ruskin "twisted geology into morality, theology,
Egyptian mythology, with fiery cuts at political economy."[10] A
question of insincerity would arise if you felt that Ruskin merely
escaped from one discipline to another without respecting the
obligations of any of them. Or if you thought he gave in to the

"incontinence of emotion" that he attributed to Byron.[11] But you would still acknowledge the sense of beauty that delights in the intrication of forms, the multiplicity of tones, and the daring with which an individual voice plays in the clutter of allusions. Otherwise you could make nothing of *Praeterita, Unto This Last, Munera Pulveris,* and *Fors Clavigera.* If you read them without a sense of a tradition alternative to Arnold's, you would think them merely ostentatious.

The question of conflicting senses of beauty arises again from a famous, or notorious, passage in *Modern Painters,* where Ruskin describes Turner's *Slavers Throwing Overboard the Dead and Dying—Typhoon Coming On* (also known as *The Slave Ship*):

It is a sunset on the Atlantic, after prolonged storm; but the storm is partially lulled, and the torn and streaming rain-clouds are moving in scarlet lines to lose themselves in the hollow of the night. The whole surface of sea included in the picture is divided into two ridges of enormous swell, not high, nor local, but a low broad heaving of the whole ocean, like the lifting of its bosom by deep-drawn breath after the torture of the storm. Between these two ridges the fire of the sunset falls along the trough of the sea, dyeing it with an awful but glorious light, the intense and lurid splendour which burns like gold, and bathes like blood. Along this fiery path and valley, the tossing waves by which the swell of the sea is restlessly divided, lift themselves in dark, indefinite, fantastic forms, each casting a faint and ghastly shadow behind it along the illumined foam. They do not rise everywhere, but three or four together in wild groups, fitfully and furiously, as the under strength of the swell compels or permits them; leaving between them treacherous spaces of level and whirling water, now lighted with green and lamp-like fire, now flashing back the gold of the declining sun, now fearfully dyed from above with the undistinguishable images of the burning clouds, which fall upon them in flakes of crimson and scarlet, and give to the reckless waves the added motion of their own fiery flying. Purple and blue, the lurid shadows of the hollow breakers are cast upon the mist of night, which gathers cold and low, advancing like the shadow of death upon the guilty ship as it labours amidst the lightning of the sea, its thin masts written upon the sky in lines of blood, girded with condemnation in that fearful hue which signs the sky with horror, and mixes its flaming blood with the sunlight, and, cast far along the desolate heave of the sepulchral waves, incarnadines the multitudinous sea. (*CW* III: 571–573)

It is an instance of what Henry James called Ruskin's "magnified rapture," implying that the rapture was dubious to the extent to which it showed signs of having been magnified.[12] There are moments in which the style seems to be leading Ruskin by the ear: "which burns like gold, and bathes like blood." The whole passage is competing with the painting. Ruskin seems frustrated by the necessity of writing one sentence and then another: the painting directs all its force at once, leaving the details to be appreciated later. Some readers have thought the Shakespearean allusion at the end pretentious, a claim made upon the most sounding tone in the English language. But the allusion is not gratuitous. In act II, scene ii Macbeth says to himself:

What hands are here? Ha! they pluck out mine eyes.
Will all great Neptune's ocean wash this blood

Clean from my hand? No, this my hand will rather
The multitudinous seas incarnadine,
Making the green one red.
(lines 59–63)

Ruskin's mind—or rather his penetrative imagination, to use
his own phrase—has entered the horror of the scene, the slavers
throwing the slaves into the sea, the slaves floundering in the
waves before drowning, the guilty hands, the sky reflecting the
crimson and scarlet in Turner's idiom of color, the typhoon of
murder, horror, and guilt. It is not by vague or loose association that Ruskin's imagination is at one with Shakespeare's and
Turner's in "great Neptune's ocean."

III

Proust does not say what the object of Ruskin's idolatry was.
He may have thought it was his style, and that Ruskin yielded
to the enchantment of his neo-Carlylean music. Or that it was
Ruskin's pride, his conviction that he could say everything at
once, as in a work of painting or of architecture, rather than
submit to the Arnoldian deliverances of prose. Or that Ruskin
thought he could hold every value in mind at the same time,
without giving privilege now to aesthetics, now to morality, law,
civil order, or politics. Modern criticism has admonished us that
it is impossible to keep our categories pure: we are told that formalism always conceals a politics, and that ontology is in a ques-
tionable relation to power; the more we think we are minding
our own business as theorists, the more profligate we are in our
exclusions and indifferences. If Ruskin's morality is predicated
on his sense of beauty and form, his idolatry is a common vice.

Proust concedes that the passage from *The Stones of Venice* is
"of great beauty," and he muses that "there is no beauty that

is entirely deceitful, because aesthetic pleasure is precisely what accompanies the discovery of a truth."[13] He recalls reading the passage for the first time in St. Mark's and feeling that the pleasure of reading it there was intense but not pure: the intensity made it difficult to recognize in Ruskin's prose the insincerities it nearly overwhelmed. In retrospect, Proust lingers over the dear and sad fantasy which he thinks he has made for himself in Ruskin's books. He convicts Ruskin of the idolatry of which he himself has been guilty. But as his meditation goes on, Proust digresses from the question of beauty by testifying to another aspect of his experience; he nearly exonerates himself by reflecting on the life-enhancing impact that Ruskin's books have had upon him, making him love the world that Ruskin has described. He contrasts Ruskin with Emerson in that respect. Emerson's thought is entirely contained in a book; it is an abstract thing, "a pure sign of itself." The object to which thought such as Ruskin's is applied is not immaterial, it is scattered over the surface of the earth; you must look for it in Pisa, Florence, Venice, the National Gallery, Rouen, Amiens, and the Swiss Alps:

> Such thought, which has an object other than itself, which has realized itself in space, thought which is no longer infinite and free, but limited and subdued, incarnated in bodies of sculptured marble, in snowy mountains, and painted countenances, is perhaps less divine than pure thought. But it makes the universe more beautiful for us, or at least certain parts of it, certain named parts, because it has touched them and introduced them to us by obliging us, if we want to understand them, to love them.[14]

Ruskin is in that sense a master. Voluntary servitude to him, according to Proust, is the beginning of freedom: "There is no better way of becoming aware of one's feelings than by trying to recreate in oneself what a master has felt."[15] For the moment, Proust is willing to forget that Ruskin's feelings may be in some degree corrupt.

Proust's critical values, at this stage in his relation to Ruskin, were primarily ethical, as he was trying to disengage himself from a master to whom he was nearly enslaved. The emphasis had to fall on an ethical consideration, the question of insincerity. But the same evidence could be produced not to further an ethical charge but to point to a psychological disability. T. S. Eliot compared Ruskin's style to F. H. Bradley's, much to Bradley's advantage. Bradley's mind was at one with itself, and therefore his style had a "greater purity and concentration of purpose." One feels, Eliot said, "that the emotional intensity of Ruskin is partly a deflection of something that was baffled in life, whereas Bradley, like Newman, is directly and wholly that which he is."[16] "Baffled" is a code-word in Eliot: it points to a predicament in which an author or a character in a play has feelings that he can't bring to a satisfactory degree of order: "Hamlet (the man) is dominated by an emotion which is inexpressible, because it is in *excess* of the facts as they appear. And the supposed identity of Hamlet with his author is genuine to this point: that Hamlet's bafflement at the absence of objective equivalent to his feelings is a prolongation of the bafflement of his creator in the face of his artistic problem."[17] Eliot's criteria, for the moment, are Arnoldian: he wants writers to coincide with themselves. Distressed by the chaos of his own feelings, he is alert to other writers similarly bewildered.

Ruskin's masters were Dante, Shakespeare, Blake, Wordsworth, Byron, Scott, Shelley, Coleridge, Carlyle, the writers of the Bible, and Turner: he learned to understand his own feelings, short of finding a form to control them, by going to school with those masters and trying to see what they saw, feel what they felt. By the time he published *The Seven Lamps of Architecture* and the first two volumes of *Modern Painters,* he had come to trust the feelings he now declared his own, and to override their opacities and contradictions. He was ready to name the principles he avowed, and to separate them in discourse more strictly than they were separable in cognition. Pater thought the effort pointless. In the preface to *Studies in the History of the Renaissance* he wrote:

> Many attempts have been made by writers on art and poetry to define beauty in the abstract, to express it in the most general terms, to find a universal formula for it. The value of such attempts has most often been in the suggestive and penetrating things said by the way. Such discussions help us very little to enjoy what has been well done in art or poetry, to discriminate between what is more and what is less excellent in them, or to use words like beauty, excellence, art, poetry, with more meaning than they would otherwise have. Beauty, like all other qualities presented to human experience, is relative; and the definition of it becomes unmeaning and useless in proportion to its abstractness. To define beauty not in the most abstract, but in the most concrete terms possible, not to find a universal formula for it, but the formula which expresses most adequately this or that special manifestation of it, is the aim of the true student of aesthetics.[18]

Pater had Ruskin in his sights, as well as the German professors of aesthetics who thought that they must define the principles of art before addressing its particles.

IV

Ruskin named the seven lamps of architecture as sacrifice, truth, power, beauty, life, memory, and obedience. In a later note he confessed to the difficulty "of keeping my Seven Lamps from becoming Eight—or Nine—or even quite a vulgar row of footlights" (*CW* VIII: 138n), but he restricted himself to seven. He does not seem to have worried that the light emitted by his several lamps might be unbounded, issuing indiscriminately from the ultimate source of light, and that his formless desires would try to return "al ciel ch' è pura luce."[19] He was concerned with the "chief conditions of right" (*CW* VIII: 167), and he was convinced that he knew exactly what they were. Each of the seven values was absolute, invariable: it could be invoked with sufficient certainty by considering the temptations it had to overcome. Truth could be appealed to by noting the rival forces of deception, concealment, and subterfuge. Ruskin shows no inclination to regard the seven values as relative or conventional, or to say, as William James did, that "'the true' . . . is only the expedient in the way of our thinking, just as 'the right' is only the expedient in the way of our behaving."[20] Ruskin was more inclined to deduce an aesthetics from a morality, or, as Proust maintained, to confound the two as if the lines of demarcation between them did not need to be sharply drawn. The process of deducing a morality or an ethics from an aesthetics became clearer in G. E. Moore and his Bloomsbury colleagues. During the years in which Ruskin's Evangelicalism was secure, he believed that the seven lamps shared the light that God created. It was enough that God said "Let there be light," and there was light. Each of the lamps was a value in practice, not an abstraction drawn from its embodiments but an idea in excess of them. Pater thought that the value was merely an abstraction, useless in any practice.

Beauty, for instance, was a lamp that Ruskin thought he could point to and rely upon for two reasons. The first was that the feeling of mankind on the subject of beauty is "universal and instinctive." In the first volume of *Modern Painters* he writes:

> Any material object which can give us pleasure in the simple contemplation of its outward qualities without any direct and definite exertion of the intellect, I call in some way, or in some degree, beautiful. Why we receive pleasure from some forms and colours, and not from others, is no more to be asked or answered than why we like sugar and dislike wormwood. The utmost subtlety of investigation will only lead us to ultimate instincts and principles of human nature, for which no farther reason can be given than the simple will of the Deity that we should be so created. (*CW* III: 109)

In *The Seven Lamps of Architecture* he said: "I shall base my present investigation on this assumption, only asserting that to be beautiful which I believe will be granted me to be so without dispute" (*CW* VIII: 139). Ruskin is writing here as a sage, not a philosopher. Presumably he accounted for disputes about the beauty of this or that object by reflecting that human nature could be perverted by bad influences. The faculty of taste as distinct from judgment, he said, is the "instinctive and instant preferring of one material object to another without any obvious reason, except that it is proper to human nature in its perfection so to do" (*CW* III: 110). It is a bold claim, even with Kant's axiom of *sensus communis* to accompany it. But Ruskin acknowledges that the faculty of taste, like the other "primary principles of our nature," may be affected by education and accident; "may be cultivated or checked, directed or diverted, gifted by right guidance with the most acute and faultless sense, or subjected by neglect to every phase of error and disease" (*CW* III: 109). The second consideration was that "whatever is in architecture fair or beautiful, is imitated from natural forms" (*CW* VIII: 101). In *Love's Meinie* he says that "the meaning of the word 'beauty' in the fine arts and in classical literature is properly restricted to those very qualities in which the locomotion of a swallow differs from that of an engine" (*CW* XXV: 45). "I do not mean to assert," Ruskin said, "that every happy arrangement of line is directly suggested by a natural object; but that all beautiful lines are adaptations of those which are commonest in the external creation. . . . Forms which are *not* taken from natural objects *must* be ugly" (*CW* VIII: 139, 141). A few pages later, he seems to draw back from these strictures. "Forms are not beautiful," he says, "*because* they are copied from Nature; only it is out of the power of man to conceive beauty without her aid" (*CW* VIII: 141). The evidence for this is the frequency with which certain natural forms appear, the work of God being what it is. Ornament in architecture "must consist of such studious arrangements of form as are imitative or suggestive of those which are commonest among natural existences, that being of course the noblest ornament which represents the highest orders of existence. . . . Imitated flowers are nobler than imitated stones" (*CW* VIII: 154). It follows that "all perfectly beautiful forms must be composed of curves; since there is hardly any common natural form in which it is possible to discern a straight line" (*CW* VIII: 145). This was true even of the Matterhorn. Mountains may appear to be peaks and spires, but they are in fact, as Ruskin hoped to demonstrate, curved and sloped forms (*CW* VI:261).[21]

If you start, as Ruskin did in his evangelical years, with the will of God and therefore with set principles of human nature, it will appear axiomatic to posit certain values without further ado. You are then likely to extend recognition of those values to consequences in other areas. Hopkins is Ruskin's associate in this respect. He takes beauty for granted in much the same way that Ruskin did—as an act of God—and he feels free to ask "To What Serves Mortal Beauty," and to answer that it "keeps warm / Men's wits to the things that are":

What do then? how meet beauty? | Merely meet it; own,
Home at heart, heaven's sweet gift; | then leave, let that alone.
Yea, wish that though, wish all, | God's better beauty, grace.[22]

The Catholic catechism says that grace is a supernatural gift bestowed on us by God for our salvation. Beauty is then a gift only less, and it points or yearns toward God's grace. In "Sunday Morning" the humanist Wallace Stevens posits that beauty is predicated not on God's better grace but on one's sense of death, as if the relation between them amounted to a psychological principle:

Death is the mother of beauty; hence from her,
Alone, shall come fulfilment to our dreams
And our desires.[23]

And in "Peter Quince at the Clavier" Stevens undoes the Platonic privilege of the Idea to the extent of saying:

Beauty is momentary in the mind—
The fitful tracing of a portal;
But in the flesh it is immortal.

The body dies; the body's beauty lives.[24]

None of these writers—Ruskin, Hopkins, or Stevens—would have thought of regarding beauty as "socially constituted."

But Ruskin found it difficult to move freely between the detail seen and the discourse of idea and principle that would ac-

commodate it, a problem Hopkins had no great trouble in sur-
mounting. Ruskin also had the problem the other way around, of
moving from the principle to the particle and keeping the circuit
intact. It is my understanding that he effected these movements
by making distinctions. It was his practice to start with the idea
or value—beauty, say—and to distinguish between its kinds or,
as in Venice, the varieties of its corruption. So we have Gothic
and Renaissance art, the diverse myths of Greece, Egypt, and
Christianity, typical beauty and vital beauty; and in other contexts we have taste true and false, the grotesque true and false,
Venice divided into its four historical periods—the first two
named to the very day. We have architecture distinguished from
building; ornament servile, constitutional, and revolutionary;
the theoretic faculty and the imaginative faculty; and within the
concept of imagination we have the imaginations associative,
penetrative, and contemplative. These and other distinctions
started the process by which Ruskin could eventually concen-
trate, single-mindedly, on something individually seen, without
specifying at every point a theory or a principle to contain it.

I think, as an example, of his description of pine trees, in the
fifth volume of *Modern Painters:*

> Other trees, tufting crag or hill, yield to the form
> and sway of the ground, clothe it with soft com-
> pliance, are partly its subjects, partly its flatterers,
> partly its comforters. But the pine rises in serene
> resistance, self-contained; nor can I ever without
> awe stay long under a great Alpine cliff, far from
> all house or work of men, looking up to its compa-
> nies of pines, as they stand on the inaccessible juts
> and perilous ledges of the enormous wall, in quiet
> multitudes, each like the shadow of the one be-
> side it—upright, fixed, spectral, as troops of ghosts

standing on the walls of Hades, not knowing each other—dumb for ever. You cannot reach them, cannot cry to them;—those trees never heard human voice; they are far above all sound but of the winds. No foot ever stirred fallen leaf of theirs. All comfortless they stand, between the two eternities of the Vacancy and the Rock: yet with such iron will, that the rock itself looks bent and shattered beside them—fragile, weak, inconsistent, compared to their dark energy of delicate life, and monotony of enchanted pride:—unnumbered, unconquerable. (*CW* VII: 105–106)

There are false notes here, the florid "unnumbered and unconquerable" coming from a tradition—Milton to Byron—that the context does not justify. The vocabulary, civic and social—"subjects," "flatterers," and "comforters," "companies," "comfortless"—rather than botanic, nearly makes Ruskin fall into the "pathetic fallacy" and the "egotistical sublime," attributing to the trees an emotion of loneliness they cannot be thought to feel. Charles Tomlinson has praised the passage for its wit—"each like the shadow of the one beside it"—and for the pull of its phrases—the shadow at the beginning, the fantasy of the ghosts, the pre-Lawrencian "dark energy of delicate life"—against the bravado at the end.[25] Proust's question about Ruskin's sincerity arises here again as a question of decorum. But one quality in the passage we can't doubt: Ruskin's sense of beauty impelled him to look at those pines as intently as anyone in the nineteenth century looked at anything. I include in this comparison Darwin, Thoreau, Hopkins, and Agassiz, even though Thoreau did not accept the claim for Ruskin. "I have just read *Modern Painters*," he wrote in his journal. "I am disappointed in not finding it a more out-of-door book, for I have heard that such was its character, but its title might have warned me. . . . He does not describe nature as Nature, but as Turner painted her, and though the work betrays that he has given a close attention to Nature, it appears to have been with an artist's and critic's design." [26] It is a hard argument to enforce. Ruskin may have started with a theory of beauty, and indeed he was an artist and a critic, but he opened his eyes to Alpine detail. His vocation did not oblige him to see the pine trees only as fulfillment of his principle. He seems to have started with the pine trees and, like Hopkins in poems and journals, trusted them to bring him home to the principle in the end.

V

A question arises at this point. Did Ruskin's sense of beauty include certain constituents while excluding others, or did it include virtually everything seen, provided it was psychologically compelling and spiritually instructive? According to my reading, it included virtually everything, and regarded nothing as a transgression if the imagination was ready to act on it. The beautiful, the picturesque, the sublime, the grotesque: the distinctions that Ruskin, like other post-Kantian aestheticians, made among these had chiefly the effect of making beauty a more capacious term. It had to be capacious, to respond to the force and the range of the imagination. If it were more narrowly construed, it would raise a question about the world and the extent of God's will in the Creation. If the aesthetic sense validated only the perception of beauty, narrowly and picturesquely considered, it would raise an issue about the sublime and the grotesque. What happens to the sense that endorses these? Is it, like the sense of beauty, a principle of human nature? Or an aberration?

If Ruskin is prepared, following the tradition of Burke, Kant, and Coleridge, to endorse the imagination as a distinctive human faculty, not the same as reason, he must extend the category of beauty to include every manifestation of imagination. Even where he distinguishes between beautiful forms and other forms predicated on the imagination, he must put up with the awkwardness of the distinction. So in meditating on the beautiful and the sublime: if he associates the beautiful with the imitation of natural forms, he must also welcome aesthetic forms that are not arrived at by that means, forms that depend for their dignity not upon nature or the imitation of nature but "upon arrangements and government received from human mind." These become "the expression of the power of that mind" and take on "sublimity high in proportion to the power expressed" (*CW* VIII: 101–102). All building, therefore, "shows man either as gathering or governing" (*CW* VIII: 102). Gathering is accepting gifts from Nature. Governing is an attribute of the sublime. "Sublimity is found," Ruskin says in the first volume of *Modern Painters*, "wherever anything elevates the mind; that is, wherever it contemplates anything above itself, and perceives it to be so." The sublime "is not distinct from what is beautiful, nor from other sources of pleasure in art, but is only a particular mode and manifestation of them" (*CW* III: 130).

The distinction between the beautiful, ordinarily perceived, and the sublime did not present Ruskin with a major difficulty: it was a standard theme. A far more testing issue was the distinction between these and the grotesque. Ruskin had to accommodate the grotesque, otherwise his claim for the imagination must be puny, he must soon come to the permissible end of it. He was always reverential toward fact, the bold existence, interest, and quality of a thing seen or heard. His drawings at Lucca, Pisa, Florence, and Venice were detailed acts of recognition and designation, instances of photographic nicety before he accepted that the camera might help him. But he conceived of the imagination as a capacity responsive to the claims of fact but unoppressed by them. Seeing is believing, but imagination is invention. If it comes to a choice between minute fidelity to the visible and the creation of a new thing, the imagination does not hesitate. Inevitably, truth being one of his lamps, Ruskin had to face the possibility that the imagination might be an impostor:

> For it might be at first thought that the whole king-dom of imagination was one of deception also. Not so: the action of the imagination is a voluntary summoning of the conceptions of things absent or impossible; and the pleasure and nobility of the imagination partly consist in its knowledge and con-templation of them as such, *i.e.* in the knowledge of their actual absence or impossibility at the mo-ment of their apparent presence or reality. When the imagination deceives, it becomes madness. It is a noble faculty so long as it confesses its own ideality; when it ceases to confess this, it is insanity. All the difference lies in the fact of the confession, in their being *no* deception. It is necessary to our rank as spiritual creatures, that we should be able to invent and to behold what is not; and to our rank as moral creatures, that we should know and confess at the same time that it is not. (*CW* VIII: 58)

This is the standard defense of fiction, interesting mainly for Ruskin's bringing forward "our rank as moral creatures" to make sure that we are not deceived by the autonomy of the fictions. Writing of Tintoretto in the second volume of *Modern Painters*, he established that autonomy yet again in terms consistent with Giovan Pietro Bellori's idea of beauty as the triumph of mind and artifice over Nature.[27] Ruskin writes:

Now, I wish the reader particularly to observe throughout all these works of Tintoret, the distinction of the Imaginative Verity from falsehood on the one hand, and from realism on the other. The power of every picture depends on the penetration of the imagination into the TRUE nature of the thing represented, and on the utter scorn of the imagination for all shackles and fetters of mere external fact that stand in the way of its suggestiveness. In the Baptism it cuts away the trunks of trees as if they were so much cloud or vapour, that it may exhibit to the thought the completed sequency of the scene; in the Massacre it covers the marble floor with visionary light, that it may strike terror into the spectator without condescending to butchery; it defies the bare fact, but creates in him the fearful feeling; in the Crucifixion it annihilates locality, and brings the palm leaves to Calvary, so only that it may bear the mind to the Mount of Olives . . . (*CW* IV: 278)

It is consistent with this passage that Ruskin regards the act of imagination not as the choice of a particular object to attend to but as "the mode of regarding the object" (*CW* IV: 227) and that he should allow notable latitude to these modes. An artist is not obliged to replicate an object or a landscape, but to add a new thing in its presence to the abundance of the world. Even when the painting appears to be a representation of an object or a landscape, Ruskin's appeal to "the TRUE nature of the thing represented" may entail two possibilities. He may claim that the reality of the thing represented is in some deep, compelling sense as it appears to a genius rather than to an ordinary pair of eyes. An artist's imagination must be allowed its independence, unless some further consideration is such as to prevail. As a rule, and without demeaning the rights of fact, Ruskin gives the artist's imagination the greater privilege. He is even prepared to endorse the dream-work of a genius, whatever forms and colors it takes. In this respect he is of Blake's party rather than Wordsworth's.

But the grotesque, like gargoyles, was still a problem. Ruskin was well disposed to it in art and poetry. He associated it, at its best, with a religious sense of mystery, the intuition of an irrefutable opacity in life, darkness at war with light as in Greek tragedy. But he felt it necessary, both in *The Stones of Venice* and in the third volume of *Modern Painters,* to distinguish between the "ignoble grotesque" and the "noble grotesque," if only because various forms of the grotesque appeared in northern Gothic art, which he cherished, and in Renaissance art, which at that point in his life he hated. The true grotesque is "the expression of the *repose* or play of a *serious* mind," but there is a false grotesque that is the result of "the *full exertion* of a *frivolous* one" (*CW* XI: 170). The distinction between these, however, is hard to show in the works themselves: in *The Stones of Venice* he has to rely on imputed differences of moral character at their source. The ignoble grotesque issues from a spirit of mockery; it is ignorant of beauty, it resorts to levity and scurrilousness, and is always without pity. Noble forms of grotesque issue from a great spirit trying to engage with the mystery of things in appalled exuberance of invention.

One of the most telling pages of *The Stones of Venice* makes the question of the grotesque clearer by juxtaposing two drawings, one of a carved head—"huge, inhuman, and monstrous," as Ruskin describes it—on the foundation of the Palazzo Corner della Regina in Venice, and another, illustrative of what Ruskin calls "that magnificent condition of fantastic imagination" typical of the Northern Gothic mind. The first is gross: it shows no sense of horror, nature, or mercy. It is "utterly devoid of invention, made merely monstrous by exaggerations of the eyeballs and cheeks, and generally characteristic of the late Renaissance grotesque of Venice" (*CW* XI: 190). He has already made a point of noting of the Venetian head that "the *teeth* are represented as *decayed*" (*CW* XI: 162). The second, a head of the lion—symbol of St. Mark from the Veronese Gothic—is "a piece of noble and inventive Gothic."

There is an even more powerful juxtaposition of two grotesques in the third volume of *Modern Painters*. Ruskin has been saying that "a fine grotesque is the expression, in a moment, by a series of symbols thrown together in bold and fearless connection, of truths which it would have taken a long time to express in any verbal way, and of which the connection is left for the beholder to work out for himself; the gaps, left or overleaped by the haste of the imagination, forming the grotesque character" (*CW* V: 132). I think he should have said "emblems" rather than "symbols." The example he gives of a fine grotesque is Spenser's portrait of "malicious Envy" in the first Book of *The Faerie Queene*. This raises the question, though Ruskin doesn't raise it, of a possible relation between allegory and the grotesque: maybe the "gaps" are to be crossed by the reader's knowledge of the particular allegorical tradition invoked. A few pages later, Ruskin reproduces two drawings of a griffin. On the left side of the page is "a piece of true grotesque, from the Lombard-Gothic," on the right, an example of "false grotesque from classical (Roman) architecture." The one on the left "carries on his back one of the main pillars of the porch of the cathedral of Verona." The one on the right is "on the frieze of the temple of Antoninus and Faustina at Rome, much celebrated by Renaissance and bad modern architects" (*CW* V: 141). Ruskin's discrimination of the griffins is one of his most convincing essays in practical criticism. It demonstrates that the sculptor of the classical griffin merely put together, in entirely mechanical fashion, diverse attributes of lion and eagle. The Lombardic sculptor "did really see a griffin in his imagination, and carved it from the life." Remember, Ruskin says, that the griffin, "though part lion and part eagle, has the united *power of both.*" "He is not merely a bit of lion and a bit of eagle, but whole lion incorporate with whole eagle" (*CW* V:142). Ruskin's extraordinary analysis shows what this incorporation entails and how it is achieved in the Lombardic sculpture. What emerges, yet again, is the unquestionable primacy of the imagination.

VI

Some emphasis along these lines is necessary if we are to make sense of Ruskin's relation to Turner's paintings. If you were to recite the commonplaces of Ruskin's social values, you would not expect his advocacy of Turner's paintings to be so intense: you would think of other painters as meriting his greater praise. Everybody agrees that Ruskin hated the products of the Industrial Revolution, including the railways on which he reluctantly traveled. He despised the perfect finish of shapes turned out by machines, and loved the imperfection of surface in which he saw evidence of a hand and fingers at work. In *Fors Clavigera* he spent years urging "the workmen and labourers of Great Britain" to hold on to rural and agricultural values: "and no moving of machinery by fire" (*CW* XXIX: 86). He was enraged to see the destruction of English landscapes and the hideousness, as it seemed to him, of modern English architecture. His favorite type of beauty featured "effects of calm and luminous distance . . . the still small voice of the level twilight behind purple hills, or the scarlet arch of dawn over the dark troublous-edged sea" (*CW* IV: 80). He maintained that *Modern Painters* "taught the claim of all lower nature on the hearts of men; of the rock, and wave, and herb, as a part of their necessary spirit life; in all that I now bid you to do, to dress the earth and keep it, I am fulfilling what I then began." *The Stones of Venice* "taught the laws of constructive Art, and the dependence of all human work or edifice, for its beauty, on the happy life of the workman" (*CW* XXIX: 137).

Given these passions, you would expect that Ruskin would endorse the styles of Gainsborough and Constable in England and of Canaletto in Venice. In fact, he nearly dismissed them. In the first volume of *Modern Painters* his praise of Gainsborough is so doggedly qualified that it hardly survives a paragraph. Constable had some merit, but "I have never seen any work of his in which there were any signs of his being able to draw" (*CW* III: 191). "Constable perceives in a landscape that the grass is wet, the meadows flat, and the boughs shady; that is to say, about as much as, I suppose, might in general be apprehended, between them, by an intelligent fawn, and a skylark" (*CW* V: 172). As for Canaletto: he "possesses no virtue except that of dexterous imitation of commonplace light and shade" (*CW* III: 216).

> The bargeman and the bricklayer probably see no more in Venice than Canaletti gives—heaps of earth and mortar, with water between—and are just as capable of appreciating the facts of sunlight and shadow, by which he deceives us, as the most educated of us all. But what more there is in Venice than brick and stone—what there is of mystery and death, and memory and beauty—what there is to be learned or lamented, to be loved or wept—we look for to Canaletti in vain. (*CW* III: 255–256)

As always, the criterion is Turner: "Yes, Mr. Turner, we are in Venice now":

> Detail after detail, thought beyond thought, you find and feel them through the radiant mystery, inexhaustible as indistinct, beautiful, but never all revealed; secret in fulness, confused in symmetry, as nature herself is to the bewildered and foiled glance, giving out of that indistinctness, and through that confusion, the perpetual newness of the infinite, and the beautiful. (*CW* III: 257)

This rhapsody explains why Ruskin admires Turner's landscapes of England, France, Switzerland, and Italy, but it doesn't accommodate those paintings in which Turner acknowledges—without any visible distaste—the world of historical and industrial change.

Michel Serres is our best guide to this aspect of Turner. He has chosen Turner as the representative painter of the moment in which fire and its power supplanted wind and water, horses and men as source and origin of force; the moment in which geometry and line were superseded by dynamics. Turner does not merely see this change from the outside, his imagination enters the boiler, the furnace, the firebox:

> Matter is no longer left in the prison of diagram. Fire dissolves it, makes it vibrate, tremble, oscillate, makes it explode into *clouds*. . . . The boiler's fire atomizes matter and gives it over to chance, which has always been its master. Boltzmann will soon understand it, but Turner, in his own domain, understood it before him. Turner enters full force into the swarming cage of Maxwell's demons. Garrard tarried in Poinsot's motion. Turner gives him-

self over to brownian motion. He passes from the
rationalized real, from the abstract or mathematical
real, to the burgeoning real that radiates from the
furnace where edges collapse. Again, again, color-
matter triumphs over drawing with geometric
edges.[28]

Color asserts itself over line and virtually makes an ontologi-
cal, not merely a decorative, claim. Serres emphasizes that the
furnace is the engine for going back toward chaos. To smelt is
"to rediscover chance as fundamental." Beneath the geometrical
forms of matter, "stochastic disorder reigns supreme."[29]

These are Serres's terms, not Ruskin's. They refer only to a
few of Turner's paintings, but those few are among his greatest achievements. Ruskin had little to say of them, presumably
because the curves of the natural world played no part in their
invention. He evidently did not like to think of statics and dynamics, the fate of line, the poetics of fire, smelting, the furnace and the steam-engine. When he allowed his mind to move
among stirring images, they were images of mazes and labyrinths, Theseus, Ariadne, the Minotaur, and Daedalus. In *Notes
on the Turner Gallery at Marlborough House* he memorably celebrated *The "Fighting Temeraire."* He declared *The Slave Ship*
Turner's greatest single work, featuring "the power, majesty, and
deathfulness of the open, deep, illimitable sea" (*CW* III: 573).
But he never discussed in detail "Rain, Steam and Speed," one
of Turner's greatest paintings of industrial modern life. Presumably he had to draw the line of his recognitions somewhere, but
his silence is strange. True, most of Turner's paintings are un-
problematic, but the problematic ones are not only his acknowledgments of railways and the steam engine. His paintings of
cloud-formations and snowstorms seem to intuit the beginning
of the world and the slow emergence of form from chaos and

chance. Ruskin knew that Turner was more susceptible to the new forms of energy than he was, and when he wrote of Turner's paintings he thought first of his landscapes. But he understood that Turner was not solely a landscape painter or comparable to his colleagues in that way. Ruskin put his trust in Turner's daimon and hardly dared to ask, beyond a certain point of elucidation, how the force of it was exerted.

One of the most remarkable acknowledgments of Turner's daimon is in the fourth volume of *Modern Painters*. Ruskin drew a sketch of the narrow gorge above Faido, on the descent of the St. Gothard toward Italy. He asked Turner to draw the same scene. Then he compared the two, noting what Turner left out and what he changed. Examining the drawings in *Modern Painters*, Ruskin finds himself saying that Turner "thought" this or "introduced" that: "But, strictly speaking, he does not think at all. If he thought, he would instantly go wrong; it is only the clumsy and uninventive artist who thinks. All these changes come into his head involuntarily; an entirely imperative dream, crying, 'Thus it must be,' has taken possession of him; he can see, and do, no otherwise than as the dream directs" (*CW* VI: 38). In drawing the Pass of Faido, one of the instructions the dream gave Turner was that he should insert a postchaise with small ponies and post-boy at the turn of the road; an imperative of genius, Ruskin says. "The dream insisted particularly upon the great fact of its having come by the road." He continues: "The torrent was wild, the storms were wonderful; but the most wonderful thing of all was how we ourselves, the dream and I, ever got here" (*CW* VI: 38). It is a mark of Ruskin's critical genius that he thought of Turner's dream as a figure, at once peremptory and unobtrusive, in the postchaise. The imperative dream directed Turner to his greatest paintings, even to those that Ruskin could not bring himself to address. Beauty and "the dream" were to him one and the same.

VII

What has happened to beauty as a value since Ruskin presented it as one of his lamps? For a time, Ruskin, Morris, Pater, and Wilde invoked it to make Victorian culture, so far as it was materialistic and avaricious, feel ashamed of itself. *Fors Clavigera* was the most explicit attempt in that way. Ruskin's praise of Morris, Holman Hunt, Millais, Watts, Burne-Jones and the impulse of the Pre-Raphaelites also worked to suggest—as the recognition of Japanese and other oriental styles did—that Victorian society would be improved, its philistinism modified, by admitting the claims of other cultures and values. These efforts may have had some effect in making a few people long for a better life than that provided by Victorian empire-building and money-making. But societies are not as stupid as they appear. Within a relatively short time, Victorian culture saw that it could appropriate forms of beauty for its material purposes and that it could quietly provide a category—"arts and crafts"— for the things that Ruskin and Morris could be thought of as approving. The manufacturers of Pears soap advertised their product by a drawing of Mrs. Georgina Weldon's face, the date May 24, 1887, and the legend: "I am fifty today but thanks to Pears soap my complexion is only seventeen."

It may be true, as Adorno says, that "works become beautiful by the force of their opposition to what simply exists."[30] But that opposition may be neutralized by suffusing what simply exists with beautiful images. L'Oréal hair products are sold on TV by showing beautiful women delighting in them. Art museums know how to sell their pictures by invoking the aid of the media and the marketplace. The reconciliation of aesthetic values with material values is indeed specious. The melancholy of art, as Adorno says, is that "it achieves an unreal reconciliation at the price of real reconciliation."[31] The relation between commerce and beauty settled down into domestic comfort so easily that artists who thought of themselves as modern—Kafka, Eliot, Picasso—yielded up the beautiful to the common culture and resorted to the sublime and, as I maintain, to the grotesque. They still committed themselves to the beautiful, as T. J. Clark asserts. Eliot must have written "La Figlia che Piange" and "Marina" in that spirit. But these artists also put the beautiful under the strain of the ugly and the grotesque, as Eliot did in "Sweeney Agonistes." Kafka's "In the Penal Colony," Eliot's "Sweeney Erect," Picasso's transgressive bodies, and Francis Bacon's paintings of cardinals in cages testify to the ugly sublime. Adorno approves of this strategy: "The ascendancy of the sublime is one with art's compulsion that fundamental contradictions not be covered up but fought through in themselves; reconciliation for them is not the result of the conflict but exclusively that the conflict becomes eloquent."[32] In *The Philosophy of Modern Music* Adorno praises Webern, Alban Berg, and Schönberg's *Pierrot Lunaire* rather than Stravinsky's *Rite of Spring*. Stravinsky is merely a pasticheur, an anthologist, adept of charm. The question of Modernism is: does the conflict become eloquent, or has it been smoothed away in deference to the high bourgeoisie? Fredric Jameson has argued that this story has a further chapter. He agrees with Adorno that Modernism is to be identified with the sublime. It follows that "the art whose 'end' Hegel foresaw is, in the light of Kant, to be identified as Beauty."[33] The supersession of beauty as a value is accompanied by the low-level persistence and reproduction of any number of secondary forms of the beautiful as decoration, "without any claim to truth or to a special relationship with the Absolute."[34] Jameson maintains that the function of the sublime in Modernism has been taken over by theory and that beauty in the easy forms of decoration has returned as a source of pleasure and gratification. It seems implausible to me that theory belongs to the history of art,

but the return of beauty in postmodernism is clear. Andy War-
hol's Marilyn Monroe, George Segal's sculptures, Ed Ruscha's
"Optics," and David Hockney's paintings of swimming pools
and boys in Tarzana are epitomes of charm. They make no pre-
tentions to the Absolute, the redemption of time, or any other
aspirations of Modernism. They are content to be charming and
to take their places without acrimony in societies given over to
the abundance of images and other commodities.

But if our survey were to begin with Kant rather than with
Adorno and Jameson, other considerations would arise. In the
Critique of Judgment Kant released art and the beautiful from
linguistic control. He allowed one to think that the object and
the pleasure one takes in looking at it are exempt from conceptual determination. It soon emerges that this applies only
to the kind of beauty Kant calls free (*pulchritudo vaga*) rather
than dependent (*pulchritudo adhaerens*). But even in this qualified form, Kant's release of beauty from conceptual control was
crucial to the development of an avant-garde in the nineteenth
century: the independence of art from representational, social,
political, religious, economic, and other imperatives had to be
achieved and maintained. It is hard to believe that this independence might now be given up. But many contemporary critics evidently resent the independence of art and want to bring
beauty under the rule of concepts again, especially political concepts. To be as fair to these critics as I can be: they may feel
that the autonomy of art and beauty has been achieved at an
exorbitant price. J. M. Bernstein has maintained that in modernity, "beauty is not only alienated from truth, but grieves its loss;
modernity is the site of beauty bereaved—bereaved of truth."
More: "What is mourned in the experience of beauty as such
is the separation of beauty from truth and goodness."[35] This
sounds like Balthasar, except that the comprehensive fellowship
of truth, goodness, and beauty is deemed to be political, not

theological. Elaine Scarry evidently wants to make discussion of beauty respectable again by claiming that beautiful objects incite us to a renewed respect for truth and justice.[36] It seems to me a poor defense of beauty to isolate it and then make it an instrument in the advance of other values. Perhaps the sense of intrinsic value and the sense of disinterestedness are lost not only in bourgeois society but in an academy that has resigned itself to making peace with its bourgeois masters.

VIII

Where does this leave Ruskin and the demanding forms of beauty for which he fought? Mostly, it leaves him in the detritus of historical failure, and it leaves beauty wherever we allow ourselves to find it. Ruskin has not convinced anyone that Venice is a mere ruin or that to see it right we must imagine it as it was six hundred years ago. Henry James called Ruskin's writings on Venice—especially *St. Mark's Rest*—"aids to depression," the work of an angry governess. As late as 1909, James thought an hour of the Lagoon "worth a hundred pages of demoralized prose."[37] Even after the catastrophes of flood, most people continue to think of Venice as E. M. Forster's Fielding in *A Passage to India* thought of it, having left Chandrapore:

> As he landed on the piazzetta a cup of beauty was lifted to his lips, and he drank with a sense of disloyalty. The buildings of Venice, like the mountains of Crete and the fields of Egypt, stood in the right place, whereas in poor India everything was placed wrong. He had forgotten the beauty of form among idol temples and lumpy hills; indeed, without form, how can there be beauty? Form stammered here and there in a mosque, became rigid through nervous-

ness even, but oh these Italian churches! San Giorgio standing on the island which could scarcely have risen from the waves without it, the Salute holding the entrance of a canal which, but for it, would not be the Grand Canal! In the old undergraduate days he had wrapped himself up in the many-coloured blanket of St. Mark's, but something more precious than mosaics and marbles were offered to him now: the harmony between the works of man and the earth that upholds them, the civilization that has escaped muddle, the spirit in a reasonable form, with flesh and blood subsisting.[38]

Forster's worship of the Mediterranean as the worthy human norm may be thought naive. But there it is, vigorous in sentiment and conviction. Ruskin has not shamed it away. He has not convinced anyone that the Byzantine and medieval Northern Gothic is morally and aesthetically superior to Renaissance art. Vasari, Winckelmann, and Pater have won that battle. I would be surprised to hear that anyone who has given up the Christian religion is resorting to Greek and Egyptian mythology—as Ruskin did for a time[39]—in search of moral wisdom. More generally, Ruskin has not convinced many people that the best life is rural, agricultural, a life of craft and the work of one's hands. Like F. R. Leavis, he desperately went back to the wheelright's shop and denounced what Leavis called the technologico-Benthamite society. John Stuart Mill played the part in Ruskin's life that Bentham, Noel Annan, and C. P. Snow played in Leavis's: mere technocrats, purveyors of the darkness of enlightened men. Like the Agrarians of the American South, Ruskin's distracted imagination attacked in vain the culture of the machine, high and low technology. What else? He has not succeeded in teaching us the truth that the only feasible relation between agrarian and urban societies is the provisional amity of conflict, day by day, never to be decided one way or the other. His noble plan in setting up the St. George's Guild to embody a finer community than the Victorian norm was no more plausible than the utopian communities of Coleridge and his American followers. In 1928 Ezra Pound wrote, without adverting to the motor car and other instruments of pollution: "The smoke nuisance goes. I mean it is eliminated. Ruskin was well-meaning but a goose. The remedy for machines is not pastoral retrogression. The remedy for the locomotive belching soft-coal smoke is not the stage coach but the electric locomotive, such as we now use on that picturesque old-world run: Spezia, Genova, Pavia, Torino. The engineer's cab is clean as a porcelain bath-tub."[40] But in other respects Ruskin was no more a goose than Pound. Like Pound and Yeats, Ruskin has not convinced anyone that works of art are the best indication of the health or disease of a particular society, or indeed that recourse to works of art is crucial in a humane society. Hegel was right in this emphasis, for art no longer counts "as the highest mode in which truth makes an existence for itself."[41] We judge the moral quality of a society by its consideration for those who are ill or otherwise in need. Law, medicine, and insurance are more urgently necessary than art galleries and concert halls. Ruskin came to the same conclusion when he gave up art criticism for social commentary. He concluded that he must devote himself, as in a besieged city, to seeking "the best modes of getting bread and water for its multitudes" (CW V: 357).

None of these factors diminishes Ruskin. We may tire of his "mewing and moaning," as he tired of it. "It's no use always saying 'Ay de mi!' like Carlyle," he confessed to Norton.[42] But he was endlessly provoked. What remains under his name is an immense, edifying body of work, including work of Ruskin's hands and fingers—in drawings, essays, books, letters, road-works, ditches, cleared rivers. The work testifies to the force of

Ruskin's presence in his time and place, whether we think of that presence as nuisance, scandal, or transgression. Ruskin's imagination, like Henry Adams's, was incited mostly by signs of historical failure and loss. We see Adams woebegone over the loss of whatever values made Mont-Saint-Michel and Mary's church at Chartres. We see Ruskin still angry, insisting that Florence is a disaster and that the Venetians can never be forgiven. The first volume of *The Stones of Venice* is called "The Foundations," the second "The Sea-Stories," the third "The Fall." An additional chapter in the Travellers' Edition of 1877 begins: "With the words which closed Chap. III virtually ended the book which I called 'The Stones of Venice,'—meaning, the history of Venice so far as it was written in her ruins: the city itself being even then, in my eyes, dead, in the sense of the death of Jerusalem, when yet her people could love her, dead, and say, 'Thy servants think upon her stones, and it pitieth them to see her in the dust.'"[43] In that chapter Ruskin professed himself amazed "to reflect how no one has ever believed a word I said."[44] He means: never believed a word I said about Venice. So he tries again, ending the chapter with three passages quoted from his own writings on that subject. The first was the passage in *St. Mark's Rest* describing the election of a Venetian Doge in the eleventh century. The second was the extract, given in *Fors Clavigera*, from the oath of the Venetian brotherhood of St. Theodore in the thirteenth century. And the third was the passage in the last volume of *Modern Painters* describing the state of Venice in the days of Giorgione. It was as if he could not bring himself to think again about the Queen of the Sea in decline and ruin.

But Ruskin was sturdier than he generally let himself appear. Except when he was mentally ill, he was more resilient than Adams. Adams saw loss on every side, and grew so accustomed to what he saw that he had eyes for nothing else. Ruskin was beset with losses but not infatuated with loss. He was open to difficult changes of heart and mind, confessing his errors, as in his assessments of Fra Angelico, Titian, and Tintoretto. He held himself ready for discoveries, as he discovered Carpaccio's St. Ursula and could never let the sight of her go. Perhaps we should think of Ruskin as he thought of other sad captains in history, including English history, in which he named King Henry II, King Edward III, Sir John Hawkwood, Sir Thomas More, Sir Francis Drake, and Sir Richard Grenville, men occupied in "maintaining good order, and putting things to rights" (*CW* XXVII: 387). He did not succeed in either respect, but he kept his hand to the same work, and the attempt would still have immense exemplary value even if it had no success. I see him according to a motif that R. P. Blackmur arrived at by reading Ford Madox Ford's novels. If there is an image on which Ford's sensibility declared its force, Blackmur says, it is an image "of devotion to lost causes known to be lost." These causes "depend for their reality on their relation to causes not lost, much as history depends on the present which it disturbs, not for its truth but for its validity."[45] Blackmur decided that Ford never found that relation. The sensibility of his novels is identical with that of his characters: "There is no foil or relief, whether of aspiration or of form; only that terrible facility with the medium which goes with causes known to be lost."[46]

Perhaps that terrible facility with the medium is what Proust thought he saw and called it Ruskin's insincerity. We remind ourselves that for a cause not lost there was always Turner. And there might still be the Pre-Raphaelites, on the strength of a few promising, imperfect paintings by Millais and Holman Hunt's "The Light of the World." But these were not enough to give Ruskin an enabling social scene. *Fors Clavigera* was read by a few parsons but not by the workers and laborers of Great Britain to whom he thought he was sending it. Ruskin's failure to find or to imagine a sufficient relation to causes not lost means that much of his energy, his momentum, goes to make a major man, a personage, rather than a body of work that stands free of its personal circumstances. Like many other great personages, his authority is the authority of failure, and of the effort that ended only with his life.

Appendix
AFTERWORDS

Euclid alone has looked on Beauty bare.
Let all who prate of Beauty hold their peace,
And lay them prone upon the earth and cease
To ponder on themselves, the while they stare
At nothing, intricately drawn nowhere
In shapes of shifting lineage; let geese
Gabble and hiss, but heroes seek release
From dusty bondage into luminous air.
O blinding hour, O holy, terrible day,
When first the shaft into his vision shone
Of light anatomized! Euclid alone
Has looked on Beauty bare. Fortunate they
Who, though once only and then but far away,
Have heard her massive sandal set on stone.
EDNA ST. VINCENT MILLAY, untitled sonnet

Remember that the most beautiful things in the world
are the most useless; peacocks and lilies for instance.
JOHN RUSKIN, *The Stones of Venice*

If ever any beauty I did see,
Which I desired, and got, 'twas but a dream of thee.
JOHN DONNE, from "The Good-Morrow"

When I do count the clock that tells the time,
And see the brave day sunk in hideous night;
When I behold the violet past prime,
And sable curls all silver'd o'er with white;
When lofty trees I see barren of leaves
Which erst from heat did canopy the herd,
And summer's green all girded up in sheaves
Borne on the bier with white and bristly beard,
Then of thy beauty do I question make,
That thou among the wastes of time must go,
Since sweets and beauties do themselves forsake
And die as fast as they see others grow;
    And nothing 'gainst Time's scythe can make defence
    Save breed, to brave him when he takes thee hence.
WILLIAM SHAKESPEARE, Sonnet XII

Beauty is but a flower
Which wrinkles will devour;
Brightness falls from the air;
Queens have died young and fair;
Dust hath closed Helen's eye.
I am sick, I must die.
    Lord, have mercy on us!
THOMAS NASHE, from "A Litany in Time of Plague"

And then may chance thee to repent
The time that thou hast lost and spent

To cause thy lovers sigh and swoon.
Then shalt thou know beauty but lent,
And wish and want as I have done.
SIR THOMAS WYATT, from "My Lute, Awake!"

Achilles: What are you reading?
Ulysses: A strange fellow here
   Writes me: "That man, how dearly ever parted,
   How much in having, or without or in,
   Cannot make boast to have that which he hath,
   Nor feels not what he owes, but by reflection;
   As when his virtues aiming upon others
   Heat them and they retort that heat again
   To the first giver."
Achilles: This is not strange, Ulysses.
   The beauty that is borne here in the face
   The bearer knows not, but commends itself
   To others' eyes; nor doth the eye itself,
   That most pure spirit of sense, behold itself,
   Not going from itself; but eye to eye oppos'd
   Salutes each other with each other's form.
WILLIAM SHAKESPEARE, *Troilus and Cressida*

Mrs. Millamant: One's cruelty is one's power, and
   when one parts with one's cruelty, one parts with
   one's power; and when one has parted with that,
   I fancy one's old and ugly.
Mirabell: Aye, aye, suffer your cruelty to ruin the object of your power, to destroy your lover. — And

then how vain, how lost a thing you'll be? Nay, 'tis true: you are no longer handsome when you've lost your lover; your beauty dies upon the instant: for beauty is the lover's gift; 'tis he bestows your charms—your glass is all a cheat. The ugly and the old, whom the looking glass mortifies, yet after commendation can be flattered by it, and discover beauties in it: for that reflects our praises, rather than your face.

Mrs. Millamant: O, the vanity of these men! Fainall, d'ye hear him? If they did not commend us, we were not handsome! Now you must know you could not commend one, if one was not handsome. Beauty the lover's gift?—Lord, what is a lover, that it can give? Why, one makes lovers as fast as one pleases, and they live as long as one pleases, and they die as one pleases; and then if one pleases one makes more.

Mirabell: Very pretty.

WILLIAM CONGREVE, *The Way of the World*

The power of the Latin classic is in *character,* that of the Greek is in *beauty.* Now character is capable of being taught, learnt, and assimilated: beauty hardly.

MATTHEW ARNOLD, *Schools and Universities on the Continent*

Adoro la hermosura, y en la moderna estética
corté las viejas rosas del huerto de Ronsard:

mas no amo los afeites de la actual cosmética,
ni soy un ave des esas del Nuevo gay-trinar.

I adore beauty, and true to modern aesthetics
I have cut old roses from the garden of Ronsard:
But I don't love the latest thing in cosmetics,
Nor am I a bird chirping the modish airs.
ANTONIO MACHADO, from "Portrait"

Because I forgive you, yes, for everything,
I forgive you for being beautiful and generous and wise,
I forgive you, to put it simply, for being alive, and
    pardon you, in short, for being you.
KENNETH FEARING, from "Love, 20¢ the First Quarter
Mile"

                    What
ought a poem to be? Answer, *a sad
and angry consolation.* What is
the poem? What figures? Say,
a sad and angry consolation. That's
beautiful. Once more? *A sad and angry
consolation.*
GEOFFREY HILL, from *The Triumph of Love*

I do not know which to prefer,
The beauty of inflections
Or the beauty of innuendos,
The blackbird whistling
Or just after.
WALLACE STEVENS, from "Thirteen Ways of Looking
at a Blackbird"

Within this mindless vault
Lie Tristan and Isolt
Tranced in each other's beauties.
They had no other duties.
J. V. CUNNINGHAM, from "Four Epigrams"

Hyd, Absolon, thy gilte tresses clere;
Ester. Ley thou thy meknesse al adown;
Hyd, Jonathas, al thy friendly manere;
Penalopee and Marcia Catoun,
Make of youre wifhod no comparysoun;
Hyde ye youre beautes, Ysoude and Eleyne:
My lady cometh, that al this may disteyne.
GEOFFREY CHAUCER, from "The Legend of Good
Women"

. . . With beauty like a tightened bow, a kind
That is not natural in an age like this,
Being high and solitary and most stern.
W. B. YEATS, from "No Second Troy"

"The stars of midnight shall be dear
To her; and she shall lean her ear
In many a secret place
Where rivulets dance their wayward round,
And beauty born of murmuring sound
Shall pass into her face."
WILLIAM WORDSWORTH, from "Three Years She Grew
in Sun and Shower"

Up higher, far away, the red digital flash of date and time:
November 10 19:47 (Sun in Scorpio. City of New York).

Blue sky light had turned black, red tracks of automobiles
wound across the bridge, safety lights on brake reflectors, red on
red.

The universe hangs here, in this narrow strait, infinity and
compression caught in the hour. Space and time cannot be separated. History and futurity are now. What you remember. What
you invent. The universe curving in your gut. Put out your hand.
Kiss me. The city is a scintilla, light to light, quartz and neon of
the Brooklyn Bridge and the incandescence of the stars.

They were letting off fireworks down at the waterfront, the
sky exploding in grenades of colour. Whatever it is that pulls the
pin, that hurls you past the boundaries of your own life into a
brief and total beauty, even for a moment, it is enough.
JEANETTE WINTERSON, *Gut Symmetries*

Many people claim the aurora makes a sound, a muffled swish or
"a whistling and crackling noise, like the waving of a large flag in

a fresh gale of wind," as the explorer Samuel Hearne wrote. And some Eskimos say "the lights" will respond to a gentle whistling and come nearer. They easily evoke feelings of awe and tenderness; the most remarkable effect they seem to have, however, is to draw a viewer emotionally up and out of himself, because they throw the sky into a third dimension, on such a vast scale, in such a beautiful way, that they make the emotion of self-pity impossible.

BARRY LOPEZ, *Arctic Dreams*

Those who find ugly meanings in beautiful things are
    corrupt without being charming. This is a fault.
Those who find beautiful meanings in beautiful things
    are the cultivated. For these there is hope.
They are the elect to whom beautiful things mean only
    Beauty.
OSCAR WILDE, *The Picture of Dorian Gray*

Beauty, insofar as we abstract from the author/contemplator's self-activity, appears to be passive, naïve, and elemental. Beauty does not know itself; it cannot found and validate itself—it simply *is*. Beauty is a gift, a gift taken in abstraction from the bestower of the gift and his internally funded self-activity.

M. M. BAKHTIN, "Author and Hero in Aesthetic Activity"

Nor does this—its amazing strength, at all tend to cripple the graceful flexion of its motions; where infantileness of ease undulates through a Titanism of power. On the contrary, those motions derive their most appalling beauty from it. Real strength never impairs beauty or harmony, but it often bestows it; and in everything imposingly beautiful, strength has much to do with the magic. Take away the tied tendons that all over seem bursting from the marble in the carved Hercules, and its charm would be gone.

HERMAN MELVILLE, "The Tail," chapter 86 of *Moby-Dick*

For the past month I have been among the purest glaciers of Aesthetics—after finding Nothingness I found the Beautiful—you can't imagine in what lucid altitudes I venture.

STÉPHANE MALLARMÉ, Letter of July 1866 to Henri Cazalis

"In a world which contains the present moment," said Neville, "why discriminate? Nothing should be named lest by so doing we change it. Let it exist, this bank, this beauty, and I, for one instant, steeped in pleasure. The sun is hot. I see the river. I see trees specked and burnt in the autumn sunlight. Boats float past, through the red, through the green. Far away a bell tolls, but not for death. There are bells that ring for life. A leaf falls, from joy.

VIRGINIA WOOLF, *The Waves*

Beauty is indeed so sexual that the only incontestable works of art are those that simply show the human body in its nudity. Greek statuary, by its perseverance in remaining purely sexual, has put itself above all discussion for all eternity.

REMY DE GOURMONT, *Le Chemin de velours*

NOTES

INTRODUCTION
Words for Beauty

1. W. B. Yeats, *The Poems*, edited by Daniel Albright (London: Dent, 1990), p. 106.

2. Walter Benjamin, *Illuminations*, edited by Hannah Arendt, translated by Harry Zohn (New York: Schocken, 1968), p. 256.

3. Ibid., p. 242.

4. Cf. Edward Said, *Culture and Imperialism* (New York: Knopf, 1993) and, in reply, John Sutherland, *Is Heathcliff a Murderer? Puzzles in Nineteenth-Century Fiction* (New York: Oxford University Press, 1996).

5. Irving Howe, *A Margin of Hope: An Intellectual Autobiography* (San Diego: Harcourt Brace Jovanovich, 1982), p. 336.

6. Alexander Nehamas, "The Return of the Beautiful: Morality, Pleasure, and the Value of Uncertainty," *Journal of Aesthetics and Art Criticism* 58, no. 4 (Fall 2000): 402. Kant and Nietzsche cited in Nehamas as follows: Immanuel Kant, *Critique of Judgment*, translated by J. H. Bernard (New York: Macmillan, 1951), no. 8; Friedrich Nietzsche, *The Birth of Tragedy*, translated by Ronald Speirs (Cambridge: Cambridge University Press, 1999), sect. 15.

7. T. S. Eliot, *Selected Essays* (London: Faber and Faber, 1963), p. 24.

8. Ibid., p. 32.

9. Nathaniel Hawthorne, *Selected Tales and Sketches, 3rd ed.*, edited by Hyatt H. Waggoner (New York: Holt, Rinehart and Winston, 1970), p. 323.

10. Ibid., p. 328.

11. Ibid., p. 312.

12. Ibid., pp. 266–267.

13. Ibid., p. 269.

14. Ibid., p. 281.

15. Ibid.

16. James Joyce, *Ulysses*, edited by Hans Walter Gabler with Wolfhard

Steppe and Claus Melchior (New York: Garland, 1984), vol. 1, lines 823, 919–921, pp. 367, 373.

17. Virginia Woolf, *Mrs. Dalloway* (San Diego: Harcourt, 1981), p. 42.

18. T. S. E., review of *The Growth of Civilisation* and *The Origin of Magic and Religion*, both by W. J. Perry, *The Criterion* 2, no. 8 (July 1924): 490–491.

CHAPTER 1

Speaking of Beauty

1. Virginia Woolf, *Mrs. Dalloway* (San Diego: Harcourt, 1981), p. 163.

2. William Empson, *Argufying: Essays on Literature and Culture*, edited by John Haffenden (Iowa City: University of Iowa Press, 1987), p. 198.

3. Novalis, *Philosophical Writings*, translated and edited by Margaret Mahony Stoljar (Albany: State University of New York Press, 1997), p. 41 (emphasis in original).

4. Iris Murdoch, *Existentialists and Mystics* (London: Chatto and Windus, 1997), p. 352.

5. G. W. F. Hegel, *The Phenomenology of Mind*, translated by J. B. Baillie (New York: Harper Torchbooks, 1967), p. 93.

6. Ibid., p. 94.

7. Friedrich Schiller, *On the Aesthetic Education of Man*, translated by Reginald Snell (London: Routledge & Kegan Paul, 1954), pp. 82–83.

8. Quoted in Josephine Miles, "Values in Language; or, Where Have Goodness, Truth, and Beauty Gone?" *Critical Inquiry* 3, no. 1 (Autumn 1976): 3.

9. Ibid.

10. James Merrill, *From the First Nine: Poems, 1946–1976* (New York: Atheneum, 1982), p. 19.

11. Miles, "Values in Language," p. 10.

12. T. S. Eliot, *Collected Poems, 1909–1962* (New York: Harcourt Brace, 1984), p. 59.

13. B.H. Fairchild, "Beauty," *Southern Review* 33, no. 3 (Summer 1997): 434–441.

14. Ibid., p. 435.

15. Ibid., p. 437.

16. Ibid., pp. 440–441.

17. William Wordsworth, *Selected Poems and Prefaces*, edited by Jack Stillinger (Boston: Houghton Mifflin, 1965), p. 170.

18. Barbara Everett, "Set Upon a Golden Bough to Sing: Shakespeare's

Debt to Sidney in 'The Phoenix and Turtle,'" *Times Literary Supplement,*
no. 5107, February 16, 2001, pp. 13–15.

19. Shakespeare, *Complete Works,* edited by Hardin Craig and David
Bevington (Glenview, Ill.: Scott, Foresman, 1973), p. 464.

20. A. E. Housman, *Collected Poems and Selected Prose,* edited by
Christopher Ricks (London: Allen Lane/Penguin, 1988), p. 141.

21. Anthony Lane, "Lost Horizon," *New Yorker,* February 19–26, 2001,
p. 214.

22. Cleanth Brooks, *A Shaping Joy* (London: Methuen, 1971), p. 312.

23. William Empson, *Argufying: Essays on Literature and Culture,*
edited by John Haffenden (Iowa City: University of Iowa Press, 1987),
p. 151.

24. Housman, *Collected Poems and Selected Prose,* p. 141.

25. T. J. Clark, *Farewell to an Idea: Episodes from a History of Modernism*
(New Haven: Yale University Press, 1999), p. 113.

26. I. A. Richards, C. K. Ogden, and James Wood, *The Foundations of
Aesthetics,* 2nd ed. (New York: International Publishers, 1925), pp. 75, 80.

27. S. T. Coleridge, *Biographia Literaria,* edited by J. Shawcross
(Oxford: Oxford University Press, 1973), vol. 2, p. 259.

28. Ibid., p. 239.

29. William Hazlitt: "On Beauty," in *Works,* edited by P. P. Howe
(London: J. M. Dent, 1930), vol. 4, p. 68.

30. James Joyce, *A Portrait of the Artist as a Young Man* (New York:
Viking, 1962), pp. 207, 211.

31. Hans Urs von Balthasar, *Word and Revelation: Essays in Theology 1*
(New York: Herder and Herder, 1964), pp. 134–135.

32. Edward S. Casey, "Translator's Foreword," in Mikel Dufrenne,
The Phenomenology of Aesthetic Experience, translated by Edward S. Casey,
Albert A. Anderson, Willis Domingo, and Leon Jacobson (Evanston:
Northwestern University Press, 1973), pp. xxiii–xxiv.

33. Leonard Meyer, *The Spheres of Music* (Chicago: University of
Chicago Press, 2000), pp. 55–125.

34. Charles Baudelaire, *Les Fleurs du mal,* edited by Jacques Crepet and
Georges Blin (Paris: Librairie Jose Corte, 1950), p. 21.

35. Richards, Ogden, and Wood, *Foundations of Aesthetics,* p. 44.

36. Ibid., pp. 44–45.

37. Baudelaire, *Les Fleurs du mal,* p. 25. "Beauty, you walk on corpses,
mocking them; / Horror is charming as your other gems, / And Murder
is a trinket dancing there / Lovingly on your naked belly's skin. / You
are a candle where the mayfly dies / In flames, blessing this fire's deadly

bloom. / The panting lover bending to his love / Looks like a dying man who strokes his tomb. / What difference, then, from heaven or from hell, / O Beauty, monstrous in simplicity? / If eye, smile, step can open me the way / To find unknown, sublime infinity? / Angel or siren, spirit, I don't care, / As long as velvet eyes and perfumed head / And glimmering motions, O my queen, can make / The world less dreadful, and the time less dead." (Baudelaire, *The Flowers of Evil*, translated by James McGowan [Oxford: Oxford University Press, 1993], p. 45.)

38. Quoted ibid., p. 57.

39. Samuel Alexander, *Beauty and Other Forms of Value* (London: Macmillan, 1933) pp. 27, 35.

40. Walt Whitman, *Leaves of Grass*, edited by Sculley Bradley and Harold W. Blodgett (New York: Norton, 1973), p. 324.

41. Leonard Meyer, *The Spheres of Music* (Chicago: University of Chicago Press, 2000), p. 60n.

42. Schiller, *On the Aesthetic Education of Man*, p. 99n.

43. Ibid., p. 101.

44. Ibid., p. 106.

45. Friedrich Schiller, *On the Aesthetic Education of Man, in a Series of Letters*, edited and translated by Elizabeth M. Wilkinson and L. A. Willoughby (Oxford: Clarendon, 1967), p. 300. Quoted, with modified translation, in Paul de Man, *The Rhetoric of Romanticism* (New York: Columbia University Press, 1984), p. 263.

46. Louise M. Rosenblatt, "On the Aesthetic as the Basic Model of the Reading Process," *Bucknell Review* 26, no. 1 (1981): 21–25.

47. Robert Herrick, *Complete Poetry*, edited by J. Max Patrick (New York: New York University Press, 1963), p. 34.

48. Ibid., p. 34n.

49. T. S. Eliot, *Collected Poems, 1909–1962* (New York: Harcourt Brace, 1963), p. 199.

50. E. M. Cioran, *The Temptation to Exist*, translated by Richard Howard (Chicago: Quadrangle, 1968), p. 152.

51. Paul de Man, *The Rhetoric of Romanticism* (New York: Columbia University Press, 1984), pp. 264–265.

52. Ibid., p. 286.

53. T. J. Clark, *Farewell to an Idea: Episodes from a History of Modernism* (New Haven: Yale University Press, 1999), p. 167.

54. Ibid., p. 313.

55. Longinus, *On Great Writing (On the Sublime)*, translated by George

M. A. Grube (Indianapolis, 1991), p. 19. Quoted in Clark, Farewell to an Idea, p. 314.

56. Hans Urs von Balthasar, *The Glory of the Lord: A Theological Aesthetics*, vol. 1: *Seeing the Form*, translated by Erasmo Leiva-Merikakis (San Francisco: Ignatius, 1998), pp. 9, 11, 18.

57. Ibid., p. 70.

58. Ibid., p. 50.

59. Ibid., pp. 79, 81.

60. Ibid., p. 51.

61. Ibid., p. 234.

62. Ibid., p. 153.

63. Ibid., p. 247.

64. Ibid., p. 178.

CHAPTER 2
The Tragic Sense of Beauty

1. *William Wordsworth*, edited by Stephen Gill (Oxford: Oxford University Press, 1984), p. 262.

2. W. B. Yeats, *Autobiographies* (London: Macmillan, 1956), pp. 312–313.

3. W. B. Yeats, *Essays* (London: Macmillan, 1924), p. 238.

4. Ibid., p. 314.

5. Arthur Symons, *Poems* (London: Heinemann, 1902), vol. 2, p. 150.

6. Emily Dickinson, *Complete Poems*, edited by Thomas H. Johnson, (Boston: Little, Brown, 1960), Poem 449, p. 333.

7. Hans Urs von Balthasar, *Word and Revelation: Essays in Theology 1* (New York: Herder and Herder, 1964), p. 121.

8. Henry James, *The Princess Casamassima* (1908; New York: Scribner, 1936), vol. 2, p. 145.

9. John Ruskin, *Modern Painters*, part 9, chapter 5, quoted in John Barrell, *The Political Theory of Painting from Reynolds to Hazlitt* (New Haven: Yale University Press, 1986), pp. 338–339.

10. Jean-François Lyotard, *Lessons on the Analytic of the Sublime*, translated by Elizabeth Rottenberg (Stanford: Stanford University Press, 1994), p. 54.

11. Plotinus, *The Ethical Treatises being the Treatises of the first Ennead*, translated by Stephen MacKenna (London: Medici Society, 1926), p. 89.

12. Cicero, *Laws*, II. 656 DE, quoted in Erwin Panofsky, *Idea: A Con-*

cept in Art Theory, translated by Joseph J. S. Peake (Columbia: University of South Carolina Press, 1968), p. 12.

13. Plotinus, *Ennead,* V.8.1, quoted in Panofsky, *Idea,* p. 26.

14. William Empson, *Collected Poems* (New York: Harcourt, Brace, 1949), p. 69.

15. Cf. Umberto Eco, *Art and Beauty in the Middle Ages,* translated by Hugh Bredin (New Haven: Yale University Press, 1986), p. 15.

16. William Hogarth, *The Analysis of Beauty,* edited by Ronald Paulson (New Haven: Yale University Press, 1997), p. 19.

17. Immanuel Kant, *Critique of Judgment,* translated by J. H. Bernard (New York: Hafner, 1951), section 49, p. 157.

18. Ibid., section 18, p. 73.

19. Cf. Simon Jarvis: "Can You Imitate It?" *Times Literary Supplement,* no. 5128, July 13, 2001, p. 25.

20. Theodor Adorno, *Minima Moralia: Reflections from Damaged Life,* translated by E. F. N. Jephcott (London: NLB, 1974), pp. 224–225.

21. Jorge Luis Borges, "The Wall and Its Books," in *Labyrinths,* edited by Donald A. Yates and James E. Irby (Harmondsworth: Penguin, 1970), p. 223.

22. T. J. Clark, "In Defence of Abstract Expressionism," in Rosalind Krauss et al., editors, *October: The Second Decade, 1986–1996* (Cambridge, Mass.: MIT Press, 1997), p. 389.

23. John Crowe Ransom, "The Concrete Universal: Observations on the Understanding of Poetry," *Kenyon Review* 17, no. 3 (Summer 1955): 405.

24. Theodor W. Adorno, *Aesthetic Theory,* translated by Robert Hullot-Kentor (Minneapolis: University of Minnesota Press, 1997), pp. 79, 84.

25. Hans-Georg Gadamer, *Truth and Method* (London: Sheed and Ward, 1985), pp. 47–48.

26. Ibid., p. 49.

27. Jacques Derrida, *La vérité en peinture* (Paris: Flammarion, 1978), p. 120.

28. For a superb meditation on this quandary, see David Carroll, *Paraesthetics: Foucault, Lyotard, Derrida* (New York: Methuen, 1987), pp. 142ff.

29. Jean-François Lyotard, *The Post-Modern Condition: A Report on Knowledge,* translated by Geoff Bennington and Brian Massumi (Minneapolis: University of Minnesota, 1984), p. 81.

30. Ernst Bloch, *The Principle of Hope,* translated by Neville Plaice,

Stephen Plaice, and Paul Knight (Cambridge, Mass.: MIT Press, 1986), vol. 2, p. 808.

31. Rainer Maria Rilke, *The Duino Elegies*, translated by Leslie Norris and Alan Keele (Columbia, S.C.: Camden House, 1993), pp. 2–3: "und gesetzt selbst, es nähme / einer mich plötzlich ans Herz: ich verginge von seinem / stärkeren Dasein. Denn das Schöne ist nichts / als des Schrecklichen Anfang, den wir noch grade ertragen, / und wir bewundern es so, weil es gelassen verschmäht, uns zu zerstören" (translation modified). Cf. Marjorie Perloff, "Reading Gass Reading Rilke," *Parnassus* 25, nos. 1 and 2 (2001): 492–494.

32. George Eliot, *Middlemarch* (New York: New American Library, 1981), p. 191.

33. Iris Murdoch, *Existentialists and Mystics* (London: Chatto and Windus, 1997), p. 282.

34. Cf. *Hogarth*, Analysis of Beauty, p. xxi.

35. Ibid., p. xxxi.

36. John Dixon Hunt, *Gardens and the Picturesque: Studies in the History of Landscape Architecture* (Cambridge, Mass.: MIT Press, 1992), pp. 122–123.

37. Jane Austen, *Novels*, edited by R. W. Chapman (Oxford, 1966), vol. 2, p. 154. Quoted in Hunt, *Gardens and the Picturesque*, p. 164.

38. William Hazlitt, *Works*, edited by P. P. Howe (London: Dent, 1930–1934), vol. 18, p. 148. Quoted in Paul Magnuson, *Reading Public Romanticism* (Princeton: Princeton University Press, 1998), 191.

39. *The Letters of John Keats, 1814–1821*, edited by Hyder Edward Rollins (Cambridge, Mass.: Harvard University Press, 1958), vol. 1, p. 184.

40. Hazlitt, *Works*, vol. 16, p. 66. Quoted in Magnuson, *Reading Public Romanticism*, p. 190.

41. John Keats, *Selected Poems and Letters*, edited by Douglas Bush (Boston: Houghton Mifflin, 1959), p. 36.

42. Hazlitt, Works, vol. 18, p. 100. Quoted in Magnuson, *Reading Public Romanticism*, p. 189.

43. *Emerson in His Journals*, edited by Joel Porte (Cambridge, Mass.: Belknap Press, Harvard University Press, 1982), p. 384. Journal entry for April? 1848.

44. Adorno, *Aesthetic Theory*, p. 47.

45. Ibid., p. 51.

46. Ibid., p. 50.

47. *Selected Essays of R. P. Blackmur*, edited by Denis Donoghue (New York: Ecco, 1986), p. 143.

48. *The Levinas Reader,* edited by Sean Hand (Oxford: Basil Blackwell, 1989), p. 132.

49. Ibid., p. 164.

50. Ibid., p. 165.

51. Adorno, *Aesthetic Theory,* p. 51.

52. Nelson Goodman, *Languages of Art* (New York: Bobbs-Merrill, 1968), p. 262. Quoted in Mary Mothersill, *Beauty Restored* (Oxford: Clarendon, 1984), p. 10.

53. Michel Serres, *Hermes: Literature, Science, Philosophy,* edited by Josue V. Harari and David F. Bell (Baltimore: Johns Hopkins University Press, 1983), p. 106.

54. W. B. Yeats, *Essays and Introductions* (New York: Macmillan, 1961), p. 224.

55. Tim O'Brien, *The Things They Carried* (New York: Penguin, 1991), p. 87.

56. Fredric Jameson, *Signatures of the Visible* (London, 1990), p. 1. Quoted in Martin Jay, *Downcast Eyes: The Denigration of Vision in Twentieth-Century French Thought* (Berkeley: University of California Press, 1993), p. 589.

57. Friedrich Nietzsche, "Attempt at a Self-Criticism," *Basic Writings,* translated by Walter Kaufman (New York: Random House, 1968), p. 22.

58. Marianne Moore, *Complete Poems* (New York: Macmillan/Viking, 1981), p. 138.

59. Ernst Bloch, *The Spirit of Utopia,* translated by Anthony A. Nassar (Stanford: Stanford University Press, 2000), p. 162.

60. Ibid., p. 117.

61. Stendhal (Henri Beyle), *On Love,* translated by Philip Sidney Woolf and Cecil N. Sidney Woolf (New York: Brentano's, 1915), p. 55n.

62. Bloch, *Principle of Hope,* vol.1, p. 215.

63. Henry James, *Complete Stories, 1892–1898* (New York: Library of America, 1996), p. 524.

CHAPTER 3
Every Wrinkle the Touch of a Master

1. George Santayana, *The Sense of Beauty* (New York: Scribner, 1896), pp. 17, 37.

2. Henry James, *The Better Sort* (London: Methuen, 1903), p. 19.

3. Ibid., p. 24.

4. Ibid., p. 26.

5. Ibid., p. 32.

6. Ibid., p. 29.

7. Ralph Waldo Emerson, *Selected Writings*, edited by Brooks Atkinson (New York: Modern Library, 1950), p. 359.

8. James, *Better Sort*, p. 33.

9. Ibid., p. 35.

10. Ibid., pp. 35–36.

11. Ibid., p. 36.

12. Matthew Arnold, *Complete Prose Works*, edited by Robert H. Super (Ann Arbor: University of Michigan Press, 1960–1977), vol. 1, p. 140, and vol. 3, p. 258.

13. Walter Pater, *The Renaissance: Studies in Art and Poetry: The 1893 Text*, edited by Donald L. Hill (Berkeley: University of California Press, 1980), p. xix.

14. Santayana, *Sense of Beauty*, p. 24.

15. Pater, *Renaissance*, p. xxi.

16. Ibid., p. 98.

17. Oscar Wilde, "The Critic as Artist," in *The Works of Oscar Wilde*, edited by G. F. Maine (London, 1948), p. 969.

18. James, *Better Sort*, p. 28.

19. Roland Barthes, *Mythologies*, translated by Annette Lavers (New York: Hill and Wang, 1972), p. 56.

20. James Kirwan, *Beauty* (Manchester: Manchester University Press, 1999), p. 59.

21. Barthes, *Mythologies*, p. 56.

22. Ibid., p. 57.

CHAPTER 4

The Force of Form

1. Cf. Simon Jarvis, "Old Idolatry: Rethinking 'Ideology' and 'Materialism,'" in Michael Rossington and Ann Whitehead, editors, *Between the Psyche and the Polis* (Ashgate Press, 2001), p. 34.

2. Wallace Stevens, *Opus Posthumous* (New York: Knopf, 1989), p. 229.

3. Ibid., pp. 229–230.

4. Ibid., p. 224.

5. Wallace Stevens, *The Necessary Angel* (New York: Knopf, 1951), p. 36.

6. Wallace Stevens, *The Palm at the End of the Mind*, edited by Holly Stevens (New York: Vintage, 1972), p. 210.

7. Emmanuel Levinas, *Collected Philosophical Papers,* translated by Alphonso Lingis (Dordrecht: Martinus Nijhoff, 1987), p. 3.

8. Susanne K. Langer, *Feeling and Form* (New York: Scribner, 1953), p. 212.

9. Archibald MacLeish, "Public Speech and Private Speech in Poetry," *Yale Review* 27, no. 3 (March 1938): 537.

10. Ibid., p. 544.

11. William Empson, *Using Biography* (Cambridge, Mass.: Harvard University Press, 1984), pp. 177–178.

12. Ibid., pp. 545–546.

13. *Letters on Poetry from W. B. Yeats to Dorothy Wellesley,* introduced by Kathleen Raine (London: Oxford University Press, 1964), p. 163.

14. Ibid.

15. Ibid.

16. *The Collected Poems of W. B. Yeats* (New York: Macmillan, 1952), p. 337.

17. G. W. F. Hegel, *Phenomenology of Spirit,* translated by A. V. Miller (Oxford: Oxford University Press, 1977), p. 5.

18. Hans Urs von Balthasar, *The Glory of the Lord: A Theological Aesthetics,* vol. 1: *Seeing the Form,* translated by Erasmo Leiva-Merikakis (San Francisco: Ignatius, 1982), p. 118.

19. Cf. Marshall Brown, "Plan vs. Plot: Chapter Symmetries and the Mission of Form," *Stanford Literature Review,* Spring 1987, p. 126.

20. Quoted in Saul Friedlander, "On Kitsch," *Salmagundi,* nos. 85–86 (Winter–Spring 1990), p. 8.

21. Cyril Tourneur, *The Revenger's Tragedy,* edited by R. A. Foakes (Cambridge, Mass.: Harvard University Press, 1966), pp. 71–72 (III.v.69–79). J. A. Symonds's text in *The Best Plays of Webster and Tourneur* (Mermaid Series, 1888) has "bewildering" in place of "bewitching." This reading has no authority, but Eliot preferred it and hoped it might be the right one.

22. T. S. Eliot, *Selected Essays, 1917–1932* (London: Faber and Faber, 1932), p. 209.

23. Ibid., p. 20.

24. John Crowe Ransom, *The World's Body* (Baton Rouge: Louisiana State University Press, 1968), p. 32.

25. R. P. Blackmur, *The Lion and the Honeycomb* (London: Methuen, 1956), p. 292.

26. T. S. Eliot, *Collected Poems, 1909–1962* (New York: Harcourt Brace, 1963), p. 59.

27. Kenneth Burke, *Counter-Statement,* 2nd ed. (Los Altos, Calif.: Hermes, 1953), p. 39.

28. Ibid.

29. Gérard Genette, *Figures of Literary Discourse,* translated by Alan Sheridan (New York: Columbia University Press, 1982), p. 70.

30. Ibid., p. 71.

31. Theodor W. Adorno, *Aesthetic Theory,* translated by Robert Hullot-Kentor (Minneapolis: University of Minnesota Press, 1997), pp. 140, 142, 17.

32. Jarvis, "Old Idolatry," p. 31.

33. Brown, "Plan vs. Plot," 132.

34. Jacques Derrida, *Writing and Difference,* translated by Alan Bass (Chicago: University of Chicago Press, 1978), pp. 4–5, 27, 19, 20.

35. Umberto Eco, *The Open Work,* translated by Anna Cancogni (Cambridge, Mass.: Harvard University Press, 1989), p. 12.

36. Ibid.

37. Eliot, *Collected Poems 1909–1962,* p. 180.

38. Cf. Denis Donoghue, *England, Their England* (New York: Knopf, 1988), p. 347.

39. Frank Kermode, *The Sense of an Ending: Studies in the Theory of Fiction* (New York: Oxford University Press, 1967), pp. 57–58.

40. Paul de Man, *Blindness and Insight,* 2nd ed. (Minneapolis: University of Minnesota Press, 1992), p. 17.

41. Paul de Man, *Allegories of Reading* (New Haven: Yale University Press, 1979), pp. 26–27, 38, 40, and 51.

42. William Empson, *Seven Types of Ambiguity,* 3rd ed. (Norfolk, Conn.: New Directions, 1953), pp. 2–3.

43. de Man, *Blindness and Insight,* p. 235.

44. Ibid., p. 237.

45. Ibid., p. 241.

46. T. S. Eliot, "The Wind Sprang Up at Four O'Clock," in Eliot, *Collected Poems,* p. 148.

47. Pierre Bourdieu, *The Rules of Art: Genesis and Structure of the Literary Field,* translated by Susan Emanuel (Stanford: Stanford University Press, 1995), p. 106.

48. Ibid., p. 131.

49. Ibid., p. 132.

50. J. C. Sloane, *French Painting Between the Past and the Present: Artists, Critics, and Traditions from 1848 to 1870* (Princeton: Princeton University Press, 1951), p. 77. Quoted in Bourdieu, *Rules of Art,* p. 136.

51. Kenneth Burke, *Counter-Statement* (Chicago: University of Chicago Press, 1957), p. 31.

52. F. Scott Fitzgerald, *The Great Gatsby* (New York: Scribner, 1953), p. 2.

53. Ibid., p. 182. "Orgiastic" has been corrected to "orgastic." Cf. F. Scott Fitzgerald, *The Great Gatsby*, with notes and a preface by Matthew J. Bruccoli (New York: Scribner, 1995), p. 192.

54. Henry James, *The Art of the Novel: Critical Prefaces* (New York: Scribner, 1962), pp. 31–32.

CHAPTER 5
Ruskin, Venice, and the Fate of Beauty

1. *The Complete Works of John Ruskin,* edited by E. T. Cook and Alexander Wedderburn (London: George Allen; New York: Longmans, Green, 1903–1912), vol. 10, 1904, p. 140. Hereafter cited as *CW.*

2. Marcel Proust, *Contre Sainte-Beuve,* edited by Pierre Clarac with the collaboration of Yves Sandre (Paris: Bibliothéque de la Pléiade, 1971), pp. 129–130. Translated in Marcel Proust, *On Reading Ruskin,* edited by Jean Autret, William Burford, and Phillip J. Wolfe (New Haven: Yale University Press, 1987), p. 50.

3. Proust, *On Reading Ruskin,* p. 50.

4. Ibid., p. 51 (translated modified).

5. Ibid., p. 52 (translation modified).

6. Ibid., p. 53.

7. Byron, *The Complete Poetical Works,* edited by Jerome J. McGann (Oxford: Clarendon, 1980), vol. 11, p. 159, "Childe Harold's Pilgrimage," stanza 104, lines 935–936.

8. Northrop Frye, *Anatomy of Criticism* (Princeton: Princeton University Press, 1957), pp. 9–10.

9. Gillian Beer, *Darwin's Plots: Evolutionary Narrative in Darwin, George Eliot, and Nineteenth-Century Fiction* (London: Ark, 1985), pp. 9, 47.

10. *The Correspondence of Thomas Carlyle and Ralph Waldo Emerson,* edited by Charles Eliot Norton (Boston, 1883–1884), vol. 2, p. 388.

11. *Letters of John Ruskin to Charles Eliot Norton* (Boston: Houghton, Mifflin, 1904), 2 vols. Letter of July 11, 1869, vol. 1, p. 215.

12. Henry James, *Italian Hours* (London: Century, 1986), p. 324.

13. Proust, *On Reading Ruskin,* p. 53 (translation modified).

14. Ibid., p. 59 (translation modified).

15. Ibid., p. 60 (translation modified).

16. T. S. Eliot, *Selected Essays* (London: Faber and Faber, 1963), p. 445.

17. Ibid., p. 145.

18. Walter Pater, *Studies in the History of the Renaissance* (London: Macmillan 1873), p. vii.

19. Dante, *Paradiso,* edited by Charles S. Singleton (Princeton: Princeton University Press, 1975), Canto XXX, line 39, p. 336.

20. *The Writings of William James,* edited by John J. McDermott (Chicago: University of Chicago Press, 1977), p. 438.

21. Cf. Simon Schama, *Landscape and Memory* (New York: Knopf, 1995), p. 510.

22. *The Poems of Gerard Manley Hopkins,* edited by W. H. Gardner and N. H. Mackenzie (London: Oxford University Press, 1967), p. 98.

23. Wallace Stevens, *Collected Poems* (New York: Vintage, 1982), pp. 68–69.

24. Ibid., pp. 91–92.

25. Charles Tomlinson, "Looking Out for Wholeness," *Times Literary Supplement,* June 3, 1983, p. 575.

26. *The Writings of Henry David Thoreau: Journal,* edited by Bradford Torrey (Boston: Houghton Mifflin, 1906), vol. 10, p. 69.

27. Cf. Theodore K. Rabb, "A Beauty Beyond Nature," *Times Literary Supplement,* June 23, 2000, p. 20.

28. Michel Serres, *Hermes: Literature, Science, Philosophy,* edited by Josue V. Harari and David F. Bell (Baltimore: Johns Hopkins University Press, 1982), p. 58.

29. Ibid., p. 61.

30. Theodor W. Adorno, *Aesthetic Theory,* translated by Robert Hullot-Kentor (Minneapolis: University of Minnesota Press, 1997), p. 51.

31. Ibid., p. 52.

32. Ibid., p. 197.

33. Fredric Jameson, *The Cultural Turn: Selected Writings on the Post-Modern, 1983–1998* (London: Verso, 1998), p. 84.

34. Ibid.

35. J. M. Bernstein, *The Fate of Art: Aesthetic Alienation from Kant to Derrida and Adorno* (University Park: Pennsylvania State University Press, 1992), pp. 4, 17.

36. Elaine Scarry, *On Beauty and Being Just* (Princeton: Princeton University Press, 1999).

37. James, *Italian Hours*, p. 2.

38. E. M. Forster, *A Passage to India* (San Diego: Harcourt Brace, 1984), pp. 313–314.

39. Cf. Dinah Birch, *Ruskin's Myths* (Oxford: Clarendon, 1988), pp. 23ff.

40. Ezra Pound, *Selected Prose, 1909–1965* (London: Faber and Faber, 1973), pp. 194–195.

41. Quoted in Jameson, *Cultural Turn*, p. 82.

42. *Letters of John Ruskin to Charles Eliot Norton*, Letter of October 7, 1884, vol. 2, p. 204.

43. John Ruskin, *The Stones of Venice: Volume the Third: The Fall*, 4th ed. (Sunnyside, Orpington, Kent: George Allen, 1886), p. 199.

44. Ibid.

45. R. P. Blackmur, *Outsider at the Heart of Things*, edited by James T. Jones (Urbana: University of Illinois Press, 1989), pp. 146–147.

46. Ibid., p. 147.

INDEX

Adams, Henry, 175–76
"Adam's Curse" (Yeats), 2
Addison, Joseph, 66, 75–76
Adorno, Theodor: cruelty of the
imagination, 85; on disinterestedness, 70, 72; on fear, 82;
on form, 120–21; on Modernism, 170; on music, 170; on
Nietzsche, 81–82; on the ugly,
81–82
aesthetics: anthropology and, 73;
Christianity, 53–54; de Man on,
49–50; distance in, 84–85; in
film, 102–5; form in, 120–21;
of Hawthorne, 11–14; morality
and, 66, 72, 141–42; perception,
39, 66–67; Schiller on, 27, 41, 49;
seeing, 96–100; taste, 9–11, 62,
66, 68, 71–72, 101; theological,
52–56, 171–72; as theory, 43–44.
See also art; beauty; criticism
Aesthetic Theory (Adorno), 81–82,
83
After Virtue (MacIntyre), 25
Alexander, Samuel, 41
"Among School Children" (Yeats),
1–2
"Ancient Mariner" (Coleridge), 58
antinomianism, 114–18, 137
Arnold, Matthew, 59, 62, 96, 97,
144–45
art: Abstract Impressionism, 71;

autonomy of, 68–71; color in,
137–38, 146–48; cultural context
of, 75–76; Elgin Marbles, 78–81;
form in, 39, 120–21, 133; fusion,
83; historical context of, 78–79;
kitsch, 114–15; landscapes, 62–
64, 76–77, 167–68; nature and,
65, 72–73; politics and, 6–7, 62,
133–34; portraiture and, 90–96,
100–101; religion and, 72, 74–76,
78–79, 143–44; as reproduction,
64–65. *See also* beauty
"Artist of the Beautiful" (Hawthorne), 11–14
arts and crafts movement, 169
authority, 18, 99–100, 145
autonomy, 69–71, 81–82, 114
"Autumn of the Body" (Yeats), 59

Balthasar, Hans Urs von: on form,
114; theological aesthetics and,
52–56, 171–72; truth, virtue and
beauty, 61
Barrell, John, 62
Barthes, Roland, 102–4
Bathers (Cézanne), 50
Baudelaire, Charles, 39–41
Baumgarten, Alexander Gottlieb,
67, 83
Beardsley, Aubrey, 1, 57
beauty: adherent v. free, 67–68;
culture and, 8–9, 18, 59–60,

203

religion, 53–54, 72–76, 78–79,
143–44

Renan, Ernest, 133

"Resolution and Independence"
(Wordsworth), 57–58

Revenger's Tragedy, The (Tourneur), 116–18

Reynolds, Joshua, 38, 62, 78

Richards, I. A., 10, 36–37

Rilke, Rainer Maria, 74–75, 127–28

Rosenblatt, Louise M., 46

Rossetti, Dante Gabriel, 58–59

Rules of Art, The (Bourdieu), 133

Ruscha, Ed, 171

Ruskin, John: on aesthetics, 39,
151–54; on beauty, 144–48, 151–
54, 156–58; Bible and, 143–44;
drawings of, 159–60; feelings
and, 150–51; on Gainsborough,
165; on the grotesque, 159–60,
162–63; on the history of painting, 62–63; idolatry and, 141,
148–49; on imagination, 158–60,
163–64; industrialization and,
173–74; *Modern Painters*, 146–47,
156–57, 160–61, 163, 168; *Seven
Lamps of Architecture*, 151–54;
The Stones of Venice, 139–43, 162–
63, 166, 175; on Turner, 146–47,
164–68

Santayana, George, 97

Scarry, Elaine, 172

Scheler, Max, 99

Schiller, Friedrich: on aesthetics,
27, 41, 49; on beauty, 45–46, 107;
on freedom, 43–45, 107

Schopenhauer, Arthur, 74

sculpture, 78–81

seeing, 96–100

Segal, George, 171

Sense of an Ending, The (Kermode),
126

senses, the, 65, 67, 96–100

Serres, Michel, 84, 166–67

Seven Lamps of Architecture
(Ruskin), 151–54

Shaftesbury, Anthony Ashley, 53

Shakespeare, William, 32, 58, 124,
129–30

Shelley, Percy Bysshe, 87

Sidney, Philip, 32

Sloane, J. C., 134

social class, 2, 29, 85, 89–96, 100–
102

Spenser, Edmund, 58

Spirit of Utopia (Bloch), 86

Stenbock, Count Eric, 57

Stevens, Wallace, 88, 108–9, 119–
20, 155

Still, Clifford, 71

Stockhausen, Karlheinz, 124

Stones of Venice, The (Ruskin),
139–43, 162–63, 166, 175

Structuralism, 84, 99–100, 124

*Studies in the History of the Renais-
sance* (Pater), 60, 97, 151

sublime, the, 66, 73–75, 80, 82,
159–60

Symons, Arthur, 57, 59–60

synaesthesis, 37

Taine, Hippolyte Adolphe, 133

taste, 9–11, 62, 66, 68, 71–72, 101

Tate, Allen, 119

Tennyson, Alfred, 59

"Theses on the Philosophy of
History" (Benjamin), 5–6